MW01714816

YES!
YOU CAN DO THE TRIPLE JUMPS

Dr. Billy Ng

Marist College
Poughkeepsie, New York

Nothing But Excellence Publishers
New York

The author and/or publisher assumes no responsibility for any injuries or otherwise, accidental or non-accidental, resulting from use of this book. The purpose of this book is educational in nature, and any skater attempting to perform anything described in this book must first consider his/her own physical and mental ability and conditioning. The author and/or publisher assumes no "duty of care" whatsoever with the reader. The reader, by buying this book, takes all risks associated with the sport of figure-skating and forgoes all legal action or otherwise, against the author and/or publisher.

Library of Congress Catalog No.: 96-92025
ISBN 0-9651139-0-6
Printed in the United States of America

ACKNOWLEDGEMENTS

I would like to express my deepest heart-felt thanks to:

(1) Peter Williams for the final illustrations and for deciphering a million personal photographs,

(2) Jamin Meyers for the final layout and for deciphering a million personally written pages, and

(3) Christine Peloso for the edition of the final copy and for just being personally nice.

All of you lightened the enormous burden in producing a book of this nature.
Once again, thank you all.

PREFACE

You hold in your hands a book that can take you to the Winter Olympics, as well as let you stay beautiful and trim for life. Practice diligently and faithfully the advice given to you and this book will reward you millions of times over.

This book compiles together all the technique, grace, beauty, pain, humor, and mental and physical toughness of my whole skating life. It is written and dedicated to all figure-skaters - past, present, and future.

Table of Contents

-1-

What Can This Book Do For You?

Congratulations on buying the best book ever on figure-skating. If you follow all the advice in this book, you will be able to do tricks which seem only like a dream right now. You will be able to get spins and jumps in one-tenth the time that it takes others to learn the same spins and jumps. Eventually, you will be able to save thousands and thousands of dollars in skating lessons and ice-time.

If you are a beginner, this book will teach you how to get started. You will learn the ABC's of ice-skating. There is no better book out there to get you started. You will learn extremely fast if you follow everything listed in this book. You will progress at speeds that will amaze everybody. Friends will envy your skating ability. You will be the talk of the school or work or home. In short, everybody will admire your new-found skating ability.

If you have been skating for sometime or for many years, this book will bring you up to levels that you have dreamt of but could never do before. All the secrets of jumping and spinning will be revealed to you. The aim of this book is to ultimately make you into an Olympic caliber figure-skater. You will learn all the triple jumps. You will learn all the spins. Everything is achievable to you if you will diligently practice everything here in this book. Who knows, you may even become the future gold medalist in the next Olympic games.

If you are a parent or supporter of an ice-skater, you can use this book to help your child achieve perfection. Everything in this book is written in such a way that anybody can understand it. So can you-even if you do not skate at all! As you know, coaches are very expensive. If you use this book and really read it, then you can be a surrogate "coach" for your child. While professional coaching is still necessary and recommended, you can correct your child's mistakes and help him or her out the rest of the time. Your child will achieve perfection that much sooner if he or she is corrected under your watchful eyes all the time.

In short, this book will assist you regardless of whether you want to reach Olympic levels, just become a casual skater, or just give advice. But you must follow the instructions give in the following chapters. The chapters can be read in any order. Are you ready now to become the next gold medalist? Are you ready to embark on the most exciting sport that you can ever imagine? Are you ready to learn all the secrets of figure skating? If yes, turn that page and never ever look back again. You are on your way to becoming a champion!

-2-

Examine Yourself - Your Age

This book was written on the assumption that you want to become the best skater possible. If you do not want to become a good skater, then this book is NOT for you. You can become a bad skater all by yourself. You do not need the help of this book at all. In fact, you should throw this book away if you want to be a bad skater.

Let us now examine you. This examination will help determine whether you have any limitations that will prevent you from becoming your best.

We will start with your age. Are you 10 years old now? 20 years old? 30 years old? 50 years old? 70 years old? Age is not a problem in figure skating. You can start skating at any age. If anyone tells you otherwise, you can tell that person to buzz off and go jump into the lake. You are never too young or too old to skate. It is what you do when you skate that counts. If you go to the ice-skating rink and just talk, talk, talk, gab, gab, gab all the time, then you are not going to become very good. If you go to the skating rink and try to learn something every time, then you will improve really fast. If you are a teenager right now and somebody says that you are too old to start skating, then that person is a liar. Tell that person to shut his or her trap, otherwise you will shut it for them. You can still do all your triples if you really want to. If you are an adult beginner skater, never let any smart-ass young kid tell you that you are too old to start. They know nothing about your motivation and desire to skate. In fact, they may know NOTHING. Period. If you have been skating for a long time now but somehow could never get that double Axel to work out properly or that triple Lutz, don't despair. Help is right here in the following chapters. Never mind about that coach who gave up on you. This book will never give up on you.

Therefore, as you can see, you can be of any age and still skate. You can never be too old or too young to become an excellent skater. As stated before, if anybody tells you otherwise, they are not your friend and you should avoid them. Never listen to people who are trying to pull you down to their level of thinking. Why should you be pulled down with them to become nothing too? This is your life, so just ask them to shut up or you may just end up kicking them with your toe-picks.

-3-

Examine Yourself-
Your Physical Condition

There are three possible categories here. They are: (1) you are kind of out of shape, (2) your are in shape, or (3) you are in Olympic shape. No matter which category you fall under, you can still skate. Of course, you will probably skate better if you are in better shape. Nonetheless, I have seen overweight people throw double Axels like it were eating, and skinny people not being able to do the double Axels even if their lives depended on it.

This book will assume that you want to get into good shape. There are chapters ahead on how to get the maximum out of yourself by working out specific muscle groups. You need never to have worked out before to understand these chapters. And if you follow the instructions given to you, you will soon be on your way to having a fabulous body capable of doing fantastic things on the ice. All the exercises given to you in this book will improve your ice-skating. No exercises are given to you if they just help you put on bulk - without helping you jump up higher or spin faster. In a very short time, you will skate like those people you see on TV.

Therefore, if you are kind of out-of-shape, then this book will help you get back in shape. If you are already in shape, this book will help you do some of those difficult jumps and spins. If you are in Olympic shape, then just do what you have always been doing. However, if you still cannot get that triple Axel, maybe you are not in Olympic shape yet!

-4-

Examine Yourself - Are You Lazy?

This book cannot skate for you. You have to get up and do it for yourself. We come now to the subject of laziness. You must conquer this laziness syndrome otherwise you will never become very good.

No one is ever born lazy. But as people grow up, some people become lazy. Are you lazy? This may have resulted from other people telling you that you can never become anything. Over a long period of time, you begin to believe them and you actually think that you will never become anything. So you grow lazy. You don't want to work very hard because you think you will not succeed. You don't want to skate today because it is too hot. You don't want to skate tomorrow because it is too cold. How are you ever going to get that triple Lutz if you are just plain lazy? How are you ever going to become a beautiful skater if you are just plain lazy?

The only way to overcome this form of laziness is to ignore all people who tell you that you CANNOT. They come in all forms and backgrounds. "You cannot do this." "You cannot do that." "You cannot do that Axel." "You cannot skate." Change your thinking right now. Tell yourself that you CAN. "I can do this." "I can do that Axel." "I can skate." The moment your thinking changes, you will get a burst of enthusiasm to skate your best. You will never be lazy ever again.

The other way to overcome laziness is avoid eating too much. Many times overeating leads to laziness because all the blood is concentrating on your stomach - trying to digest all that food. Since all the blood is focused on your stomach rather than your brain, you will feel tired and lazy. You will have no Umph! to do that triple Axel. In fact, you won't even be able to do a single Axel. You will just want to lie down and go to sleep. You won't want to go to the skating rink. You won't want to drive there. If you get there, you won't want to skate. You will prefer gab, gab, gabbing with all your friends. In other words, you will be just lazy because you overate.

This book will tell you briefly what foods to eat and what to avoid later on. It will also tell you what vitamins and minerals to take so that you can push your body to the limits, yet never feel tired or lazy ever again.

-5-

You Want It When?

This book assumes that you want to do all the jumps and spins in the shortest possible time. If you want to spend the next 50 years of your life just doing one jump, then this book is not for you. All the items described here in this book came from my own personal experience and lots and lots of falls. All the secrets I have learned through the years will be revealed to you. If you learn how to do it correctly, then you can avoid months and years of doing the wrong thing. There is nothing more frustrating than learning something the wrong way for years and then having to spend years more trying to correct that mistake. And during all that time you are dishing out thousands and thousands of dollars in ice-time, lessons, etc. Is that crazy or what? In fact, if you think that there are other things you can do with your money, then welcome to the club. We are willing to pay money only if we can learn; and we do not like to pay money and then learn nothing or learn the wrong thing!

Therefore, in order to learn items as fast as possible, you must try to follow the suggestions given. Don't leave out anything. If you already can do something well, then you don't have to learn everything from scratch. Just concentrate on those items which you cannot do or are stuck on. As you read through the book, try to think and picture yourself doing the items over and over again. Make absolutely sure that you get the technique down pat. Don't leave anything to chance. Don't just go out there on the ice and throw your body about. You won't land jumps that way. Luck has nothing to do with it. It is all technique, technique, technique.

Hence, make sure you know the technique first. Go over the technique in your head. Make sure you understand it. Then go out there and do it!

-6-

Why You Skate

The end result of all your skating is to look good out there on the ice. You must remember this. Let me repeat myself, you must look good when you are skating. Otherwise, why should anybody look at you when you are skating? Remember, those people "out there" took time out and may even have paid big bucks to see you skate. So you must skate beautifully for them. Even if you cannot jump at all, you still must skate beautifully. If you can do triples, quadruples, or a zillion spins in the air, you still must look good. If all you can do are triples and you look horrible overall in your skating program, then you have missed the point in skating. Because those people "out there" can go buy a kangaroo and watch it jump too. Given enough training, the kangaroo can spin and jump too.

Therefore, you must be able to combine beautiful skating with all of your jumps. Always remind yourself that it is a privilege for you to be given the chance to skate and to perform a program in front of people. After all, they don't have to watch you skate. They can watch other people. Or they can go out and eat pizza and watch a movie. Why should they watch you when they can do so many other things? The answer is that you look good out there on the ice.

-7-

Yes, You Can Do It

All of you reading this book are at different levels of skating ability. So you may have a billion different questions as to whether you can do this triple jump, or whether you can even go backwards, or whether you can do a back flip, or ... The answer to all your questions is YES, YOU CAN DO IT.

There is nothing to stop you from becoming an Olympic skater. When you were born, nobody discovered a tattoo on your body stating that you are a third-class skater or that if you try to do a triple jump your navel will fall off. Therefore, the answer is Yes. Yes, you can start learning how to skate even if you are 100 years old. Yes, you can do that triple Lutz. Yes, you can do that outside-edge. Yes, you can become a queen or king on the ice.

However, you may have people around you who will tell you NO, YOU CANNOT DO IT. These are the people you must avoid at all costs. These are the lunatics and sad dogs who should be chained up until they correct their negative attitudes. You must never ever listen to them. Listening to them will get you down...down...down. And you will just drown with them. Why should you listen to them? They are never the best at what they do because their minds are screwed up. Their objective is to mess you up. If you listen to them, you will never take up skating, you will never do that double jump, you will never be able to spin that way, you don't have enough money, you don't have enough talent, you are took short, you are too tall, you are too thin, you are too fat, you are black, you are white, you are ... STOP THE NONSENSE NOW. Don't listen to these people. I repeat, don't listen to these people. They don't know what they are talking about. To shut them up, buy lots of pizza and force them to eat it all up. After all, they won't be able to speak if their mouths are full.

The only requirement to becoming a good skater is wanting to be a good skater. That is the only thing needed. There are no age limits, no gender limits, no race limits, no height limits, no strength limits, no anything but desire required. In fact, most of the jumps and spins are quite easy and can be learned in a short period of time. Even not-so-easy jumps and spins can still be achieved, although it will take a slightly longer period of time.

The only time a jump or spin or whatever becomes impossible is when you believe it is impossible to do it. The moment you think it is not possible, then it becomes impossible. For example, maybe you heard from someone that if you are over 20 years old, you should not consider taking up skating. What absolute rubbish! I know people who started long past their 20th birthday who can now do all the doubles. So you may have to go through a complete renewing of your mind-thought process. Mentally recondition yourself daily to believe that it is all possible.

After all, I am telling you that it is possible. Why don't you believe me instead of all those people who tell you that it is impossible? If you continue to believe in those messed up friends of yours, then I cannot help you become better. Like I said before, in order to shut them up, shove pizza or Doritos into their negative mouths.

-8-

Build Yourself Up First And Then Help Others

Unlike many other sports, you can enjoy ice-skating just by yourself. You do not need a partner to skate with (unless you want to), and you do not need to compete with any person other than yourself.

So, whenever you are ready to skate, you just skate. No need to call up some other person, no need to wait for somebody else, and definitely, no need to be dragged down if other people do not have the same talent as you have.

Ice-skating is a sport and art that builds you up as an individual. It makes you more aware of your whole body such that you will have better body posture, a more graceful head carriage, and generally a leaner and stronger physique. It develops you mentally such that you will have more perseverance, courage and overall confidence. It also helps you develop a tolerance for hard work and a never-give-up attitude that will greatly help you in school or work or home or whatever else that you do.

When you are built up as an individual, then you can reach out and help other people. It is very hard to help other people if you need major help yourself. Ice-skating greatly develops you mentally and physically such that you can, ultimately, help other people. And there is no greater satisfaction than being able to help out other people!

-9-

Yes, You Have To Work Out

While it is entirely possible to skate without ever working out, you will find that if you combine a regimen of working out with skating, your skating abilities will improve tremendously. All top athletes work out. So, what's so special about you that you do not need to work out?

The first thing that you have to know about working out is how to do exercises that simulate or closely resemble the actions you are going to take while skating. You would not, for example, try to develop a 50-inch bust line because that does not help your jumps at all. That may improve your social life, but that is not our concern here. Why do exercises that closely resemble skating movements? When you work out these muscles with weights, these same skating muscles have to work harder to do the same things. Hence, they grow stronger. Therefore, when you next skate (after working out), these same skating muscles will explode with energy because they are now stronger.

The next two chapters cover completely all the exercises you will ever need in ice-skating. The first chapter deals with lower body strength. That is most important for skating. The second chapter deals with upper body strength. That is critical if you want to do all your doubles and triples.

As you read these chapters and try the exercises described, remember that you want to lift heavy weights with just a few repetitions. This will give you the explosion necessary to accomplish the triples. Do not lift light weights many, many times. That builds muscle bulk, and that extra weight would not really help you jump higher. Remember, "heavy weights, less times," not "light weights, many times."

When competition time approaches, stop doing the heavy weights. Now you are allowed to switch over to light weights. Make sure you move faster now for quick, explosive movements. The strength you gained from doing those heavy weights will not be lost for at least a couple of weeks.

-10-

Lower Body Strength Work Out Exercises

The lower body (from tummy to legs) must be strong to do some of the harder jumps and spins. If you follow the exercises described, you will be astonished as to how easy those "hard" jumps and spins really are.

Exercise 1: Squats

This is the best exercise you can do for jumping up higher. There is no equal to this. You do not need to do a full squat to get maximum benefits. A half-squat will be enough. Make sure that your body is straight when doing the squat. There is a fantastic variation to this squat that I do. I go down a bit, then stop, and hold the position. Then I go down a bit again, stop and hold. I do this about four times before I reach the squat position pictured here. It will give you such explosion when you jump that you will be amazed.

You can also do squat jumps. With your body straight, bend your knees into a squat and jump up as high as possible. This is extremely difficult, so attempt it only after you are quite strong.

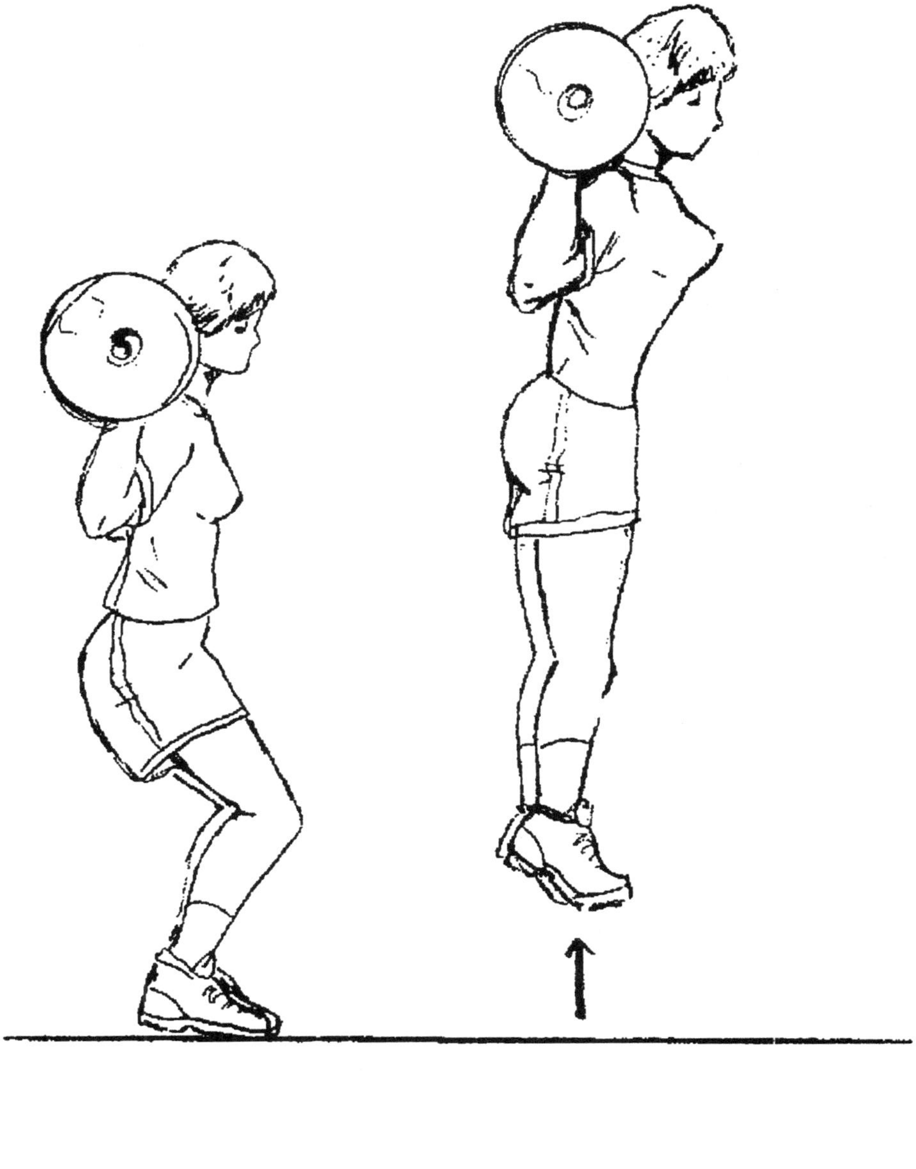

Exercise 2: Standing/Lying/Sitting Leg Presses

Here are another two very good exercises for jumping up higher. Once again, make sure that your body is straight when performing these exercises.

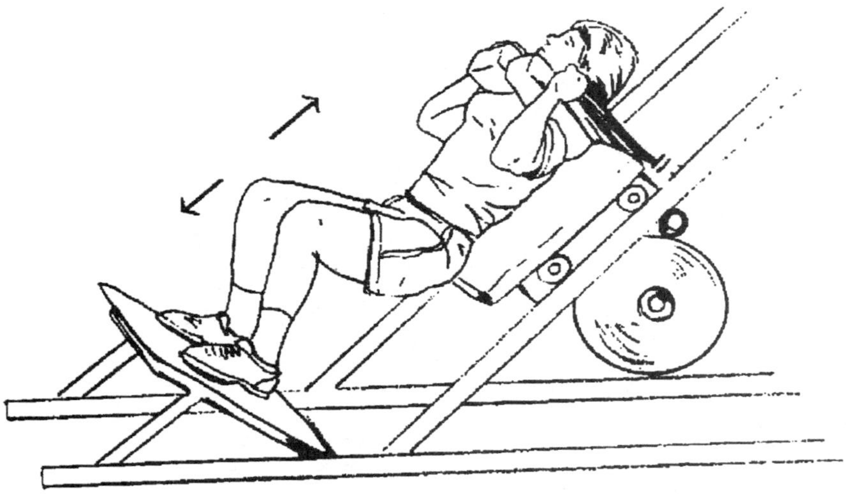

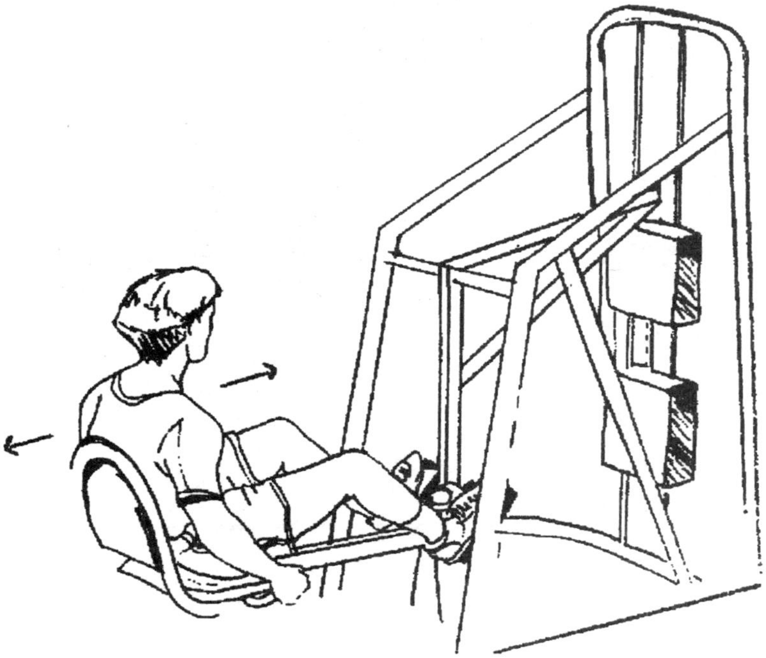

Exercise 3: Knee Extensions

I find this exercise less effective than the squat, but it still will work wonders in improving your quad muscles for higher jumps.

Exercise 4: Toe Raises

I find this exercise effective in developing the upper or larger calf muscles. If you bend your knees slightly while doing these toe raises, it will strengthen the lower or smaller calf muscle.

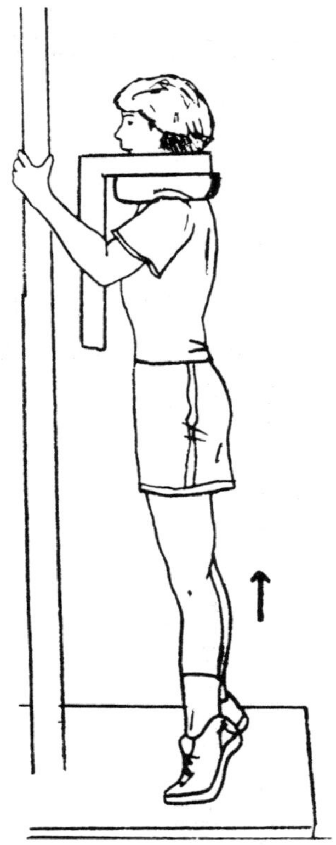

Exercise 5: Hamstring Curls

This exercise is very good for the hamstrings. If you do this exercise long enough, you will probably never have any hamstring injuries. This muscle is also essential to jumping higher.

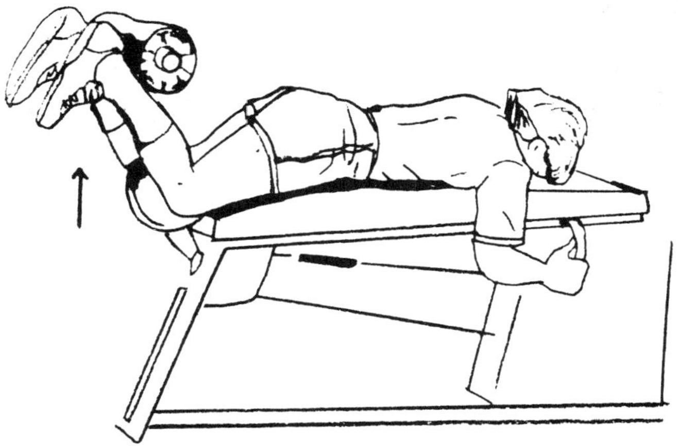

Exercise 6: Leg Curls

I like this exercise because it simulates the kicking up of the knee, e.g. in Axels. Remember, in most of your jumps, the free leg kicks up when you jump up to give you vertical height. The more powerful the kick-up, the higher the jump.

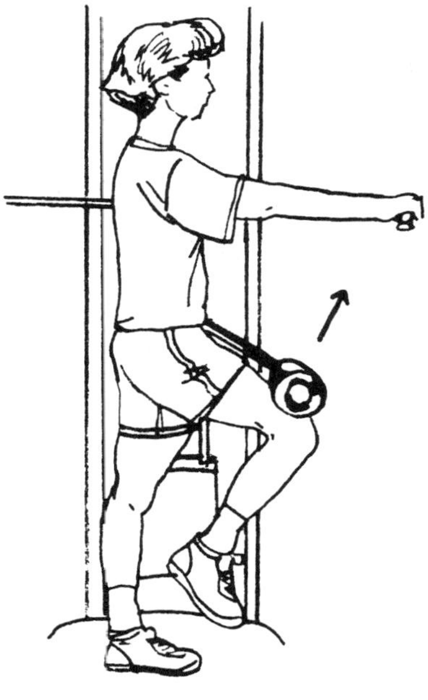

Exercise 7: Adduction Machine Exercises

These exercises help you cross your legs around each other tightly for a fast spin in the air. Always try to imagine yourself closing your legs together in the jump when doing these exercises.

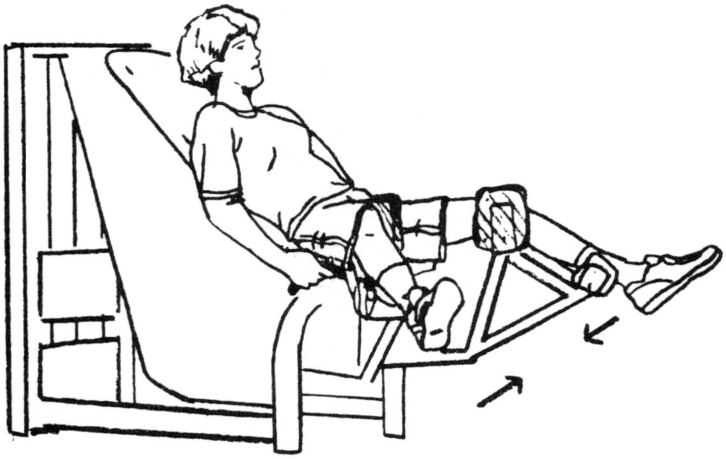

Exercise 8: Stair-Stepper

Here is the easiest method to gain leg strength. I find it not so effective because it does not give you that "explosion" that is so important in ice-skating. But it sure does build up your stamina! And you will require all that stamina in your long program.

Exercise 9: Crunches

This is the best method to get those iron stomach muscles. Do thousands of these crunches and you will never have problems with flying camels, death drops, etc. It is also crucial for the difficult jumps. You can either do crunches straight up or you can twist to the left or right as you come up. Remember, do not do Sit-Ups (this is the one where you come up all the way) as they do NOT help you. You must also try reverse crunches. Instead of raising your upper body, raise your legs until they are perpendicular to the ground. Now lower your legs to the right side. Raise them up straight again. Now lower your legs to the left side. Repeat.

Exercise 10: Hyperextension

This exercise strengthens your back muscles completely. It is extremely effective for beautiful camel spins, butterflies, etc. Try to hold one hand out, with the other hand at the back just like in a camel spin position.

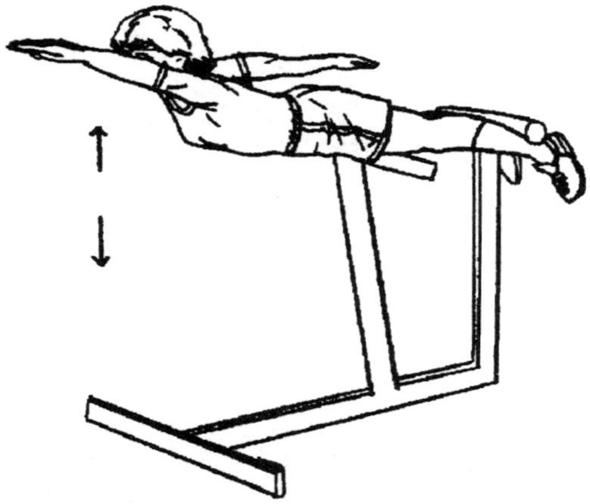

Exercise 11: Russian Twists

These two exercises will give you the aggressive twist necessary for fast spins in the air. The Russian twists start by you lying suspended on a Roman chair. Now you can start twisting to the right. Now back straight where you started. Now twist to the left. Now back where you started. This exercise is excellent for developing back, hip and side muscles.

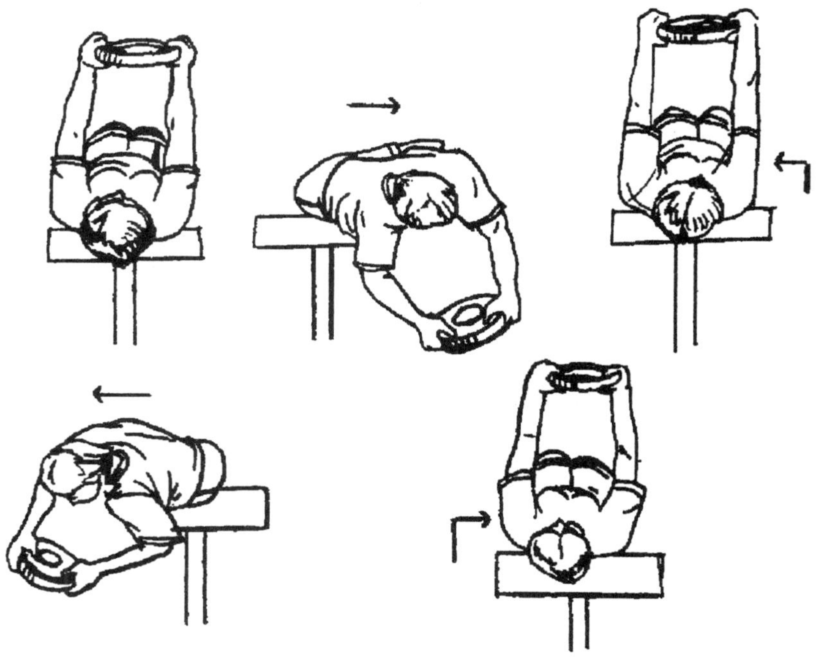

Exercise 12: Plate Swings

This exercise involves the same range of motion except that you are standing up straight. Imagine that you are twisting up into the jump as you perform this exercise.

Do all 12 exercises described here regularly to maintain peak strength. Do not do the exercises every day, but approximately three times per week.

-11-

Upper Body Strength Work Out Exercises

Yes, you need upper body strength to do the harder double jumps and the triples. These exercises will help you rotate more aggressively as you jump up. They also help you fold in tighter for a faster spin to complete all the revolutions in the air. You will find that the triple Axel is impossible if you do not have enough upper body strength.

Exercise 1: Butterfly

This exercise simulates the wrapping in of the arms for a tight spin in the air. It is excellent for tight, fast spins.

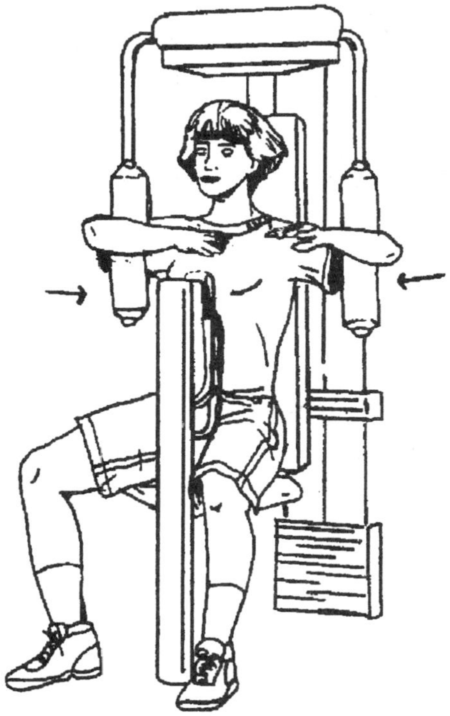

Exercise 2: Rowing

This exercise simulates the pulling in of the arms to the body immediately after jumping in the air. It also gives fast, tight spins in the air.

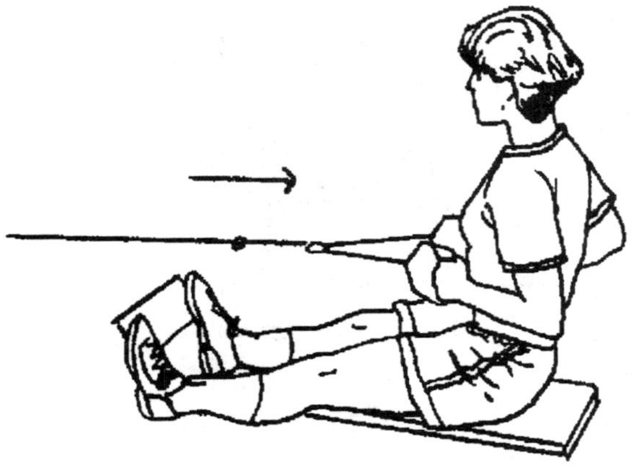

Exercise 3: Curls

This exercise develops power in the arms to thrust up during jumps. The arms must thrust up to give you maximum height in all the jumps.

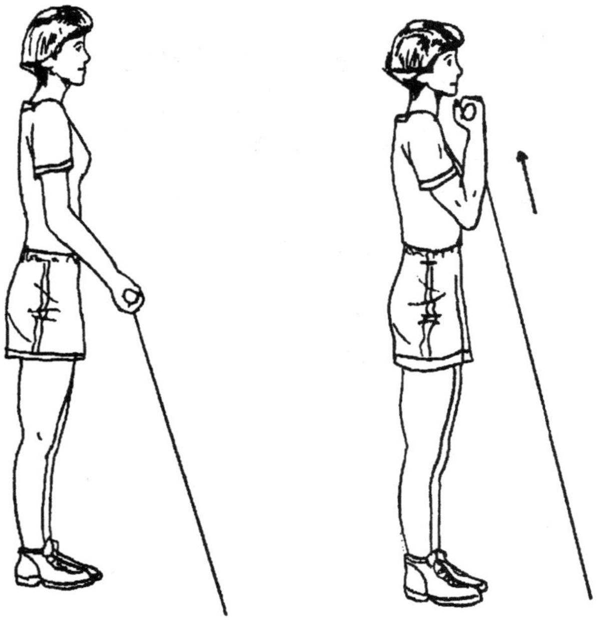

Exercise 4: Bench Press

This exercise is to help strengthen your chest muscles. This helps you spin around forcefully.

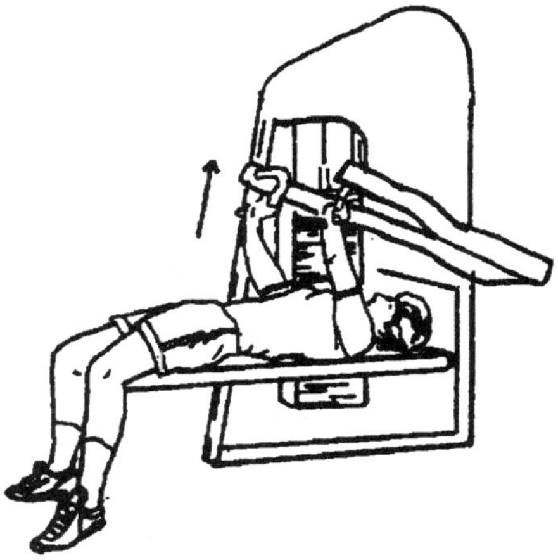

Exercise 5: Push-Ups with Explosive Fast Arms

This exercise develops the lightning fast, explosive arm actions necessary for tight spins. Place your palms on boxes. Drop down between the boxes, and as soon as your palms hit the floor, quickly explode back onto the boxes. You can even try to clap in mid-air when you get better and faster.

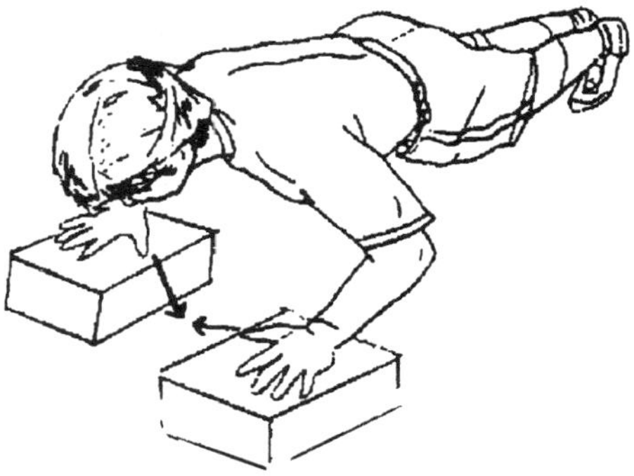

Once again, make sure you do these five exercises about three times a week. Do not do them every day. This allows your muscles to rest and become stronger the next time.

-12-

Plyometric Training OR What Was That Again?

Never mind about that funny name "plyometric." Plyometrics are just jump drills that stretch and contract (eccentric and concentric) your muscles for maximum explosions. In other words, if you follow it, you will be able to jump up 2-3 feet higher. And that is what you want, isn't it? If you ultimately jump up high enough, you will be the first person to land that quad Axel.

So, what do you have to do? Before you start plyometric exercises, make sure that you already have some leg strength. Go back and read the chapter on working out those leg muscles. Second, you must perform each exercise I describe here at maximal effort. If you are in half-a-mind, then you will not get much better. Third, always wear sneakers when you are doing the following exercises to absorb the shock from repeated jumping. Remember, the ultimate objective is to jump 2-3 feet higher.

1. Single Jumps (both legs). Jump up as high as possible with both legs. Land. And pause. Now jump up as high as possible again with both legs. Repeat. Note that there must be a pause between jumps to prevent transference of momentum from one jump to the other. Fold your arms into your chest at each takeoff. Make sure that your body and legs are straight when you are in the air. Do about 40 times.

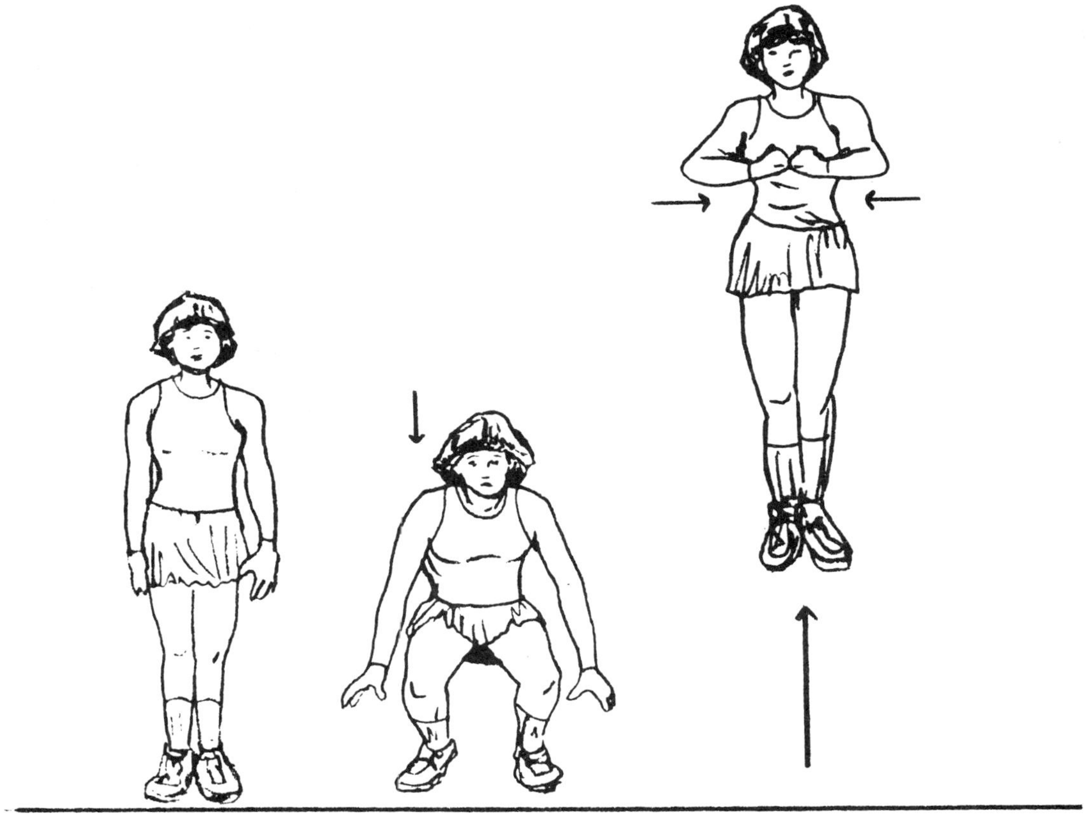

2. Single Jumps (one leg). Do the same movements except you are jumping off on one leg now. Punch upwards with both fists and fold your arms into your chest as you jump up. Kick the knee of your free leg up when you jump up. This combination of arms and free leg movement will make you "weightless" for a split second in the air. Repeat 40 times for each leg.

Right Leg Jump

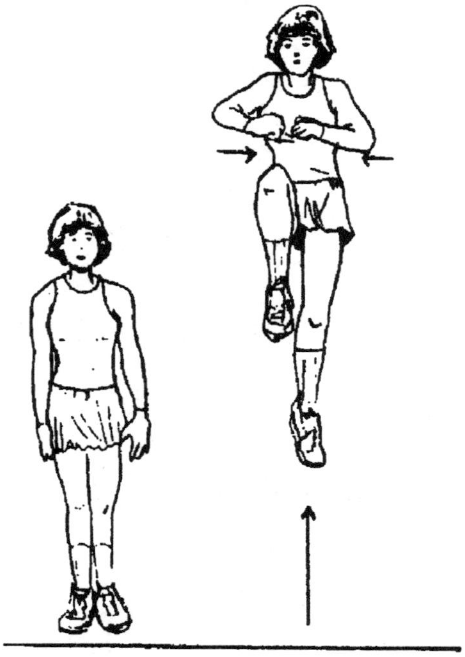

Left Leg Jump

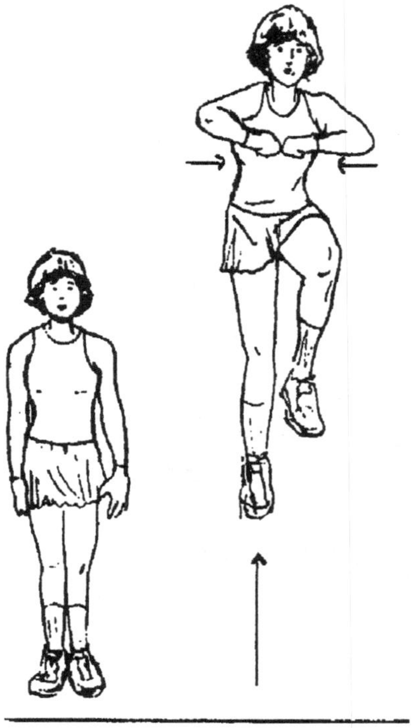

3. Multiple Jumps (both legs). Jump up as high as possible. Land. Immediately jump up again. Repeat. Note that there are now no pauses in between jumps. You use the momentum from the previous jump to help you on your next jump and so on. Repeat 50 times.

4. Hurdle jumps. I recommend three variations here. The first is where you take off on one foot, jump over the hurdle and land on the other foot. Repeat.

For example, if you take off on the left foot, then land on your right foot.

The second variation is where you take off on one foot, jump over the hurdle, and land on the same foot. Repeat.

For example, if you take off on the right foot, then land on your right foot.

The third variation is a double leg jump. Take off on two legs, jump over the hurdle and land on both legs. Repeat.

5. Box Drills. First, the boxes should be around eighteen inches square on top and should be absolutely stable and well constructed. The height of the box can range up to 4 feet. Above 4 feet, the effectiveness of this exercise will lose its meaning. You do not get any faster or more explosive at all. It is like drinking a whole bottle of medication when only one spoonful is the recommended dosage. It does more harm than good.

   Second, because these exercises are very demanding, it should be discontinued approximately 7-10 days before competition. The benefits will not diminish in that time. You will stay in peak jumping condition for approximately two weeks after stopping.

   The exercises are easy enough. You jump up and down the boxes. Follow the pattern I have described for you here. "B" stands for both feet. "R" stands for right foot only. "L" stands for left foot only.

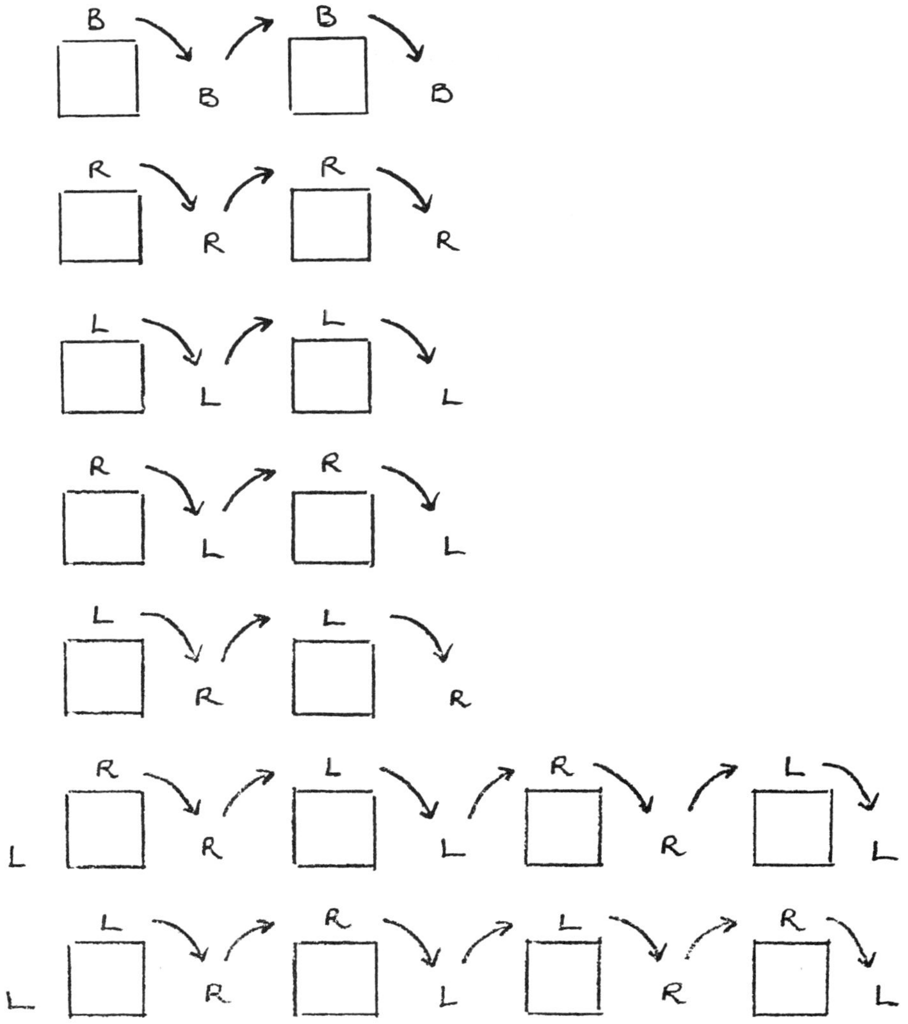

6. Depth Jumping. You jump down from a height and immediately do a rebounding jump vertically upwards (to the same height that you jumped down from). All the principles from box drills apply here. The height that you jump down from will depend upon how tall you are. Try to do a height that is about half to three-quarters your height.

With the jump exercises described here, you will discover that in a short period of time, you can add 2-3 feet height to your jumps.

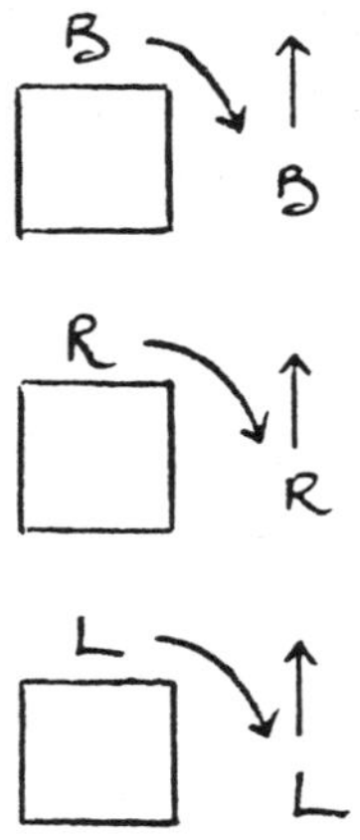

-13-

Did You Take Your Wheaties Today?

The first thing about food is that usually you cannot have too much of it. There may be times whereby you actually have to starve yourself a bit. Sounds crazy, doesn't it? But if you want the triples, then that is what you may have to do.

So what is proper food for an ice-skater? The first food to take is anything containing complex carbohydrates. Try lots of pasta, rice, potatoes, bread, muffins, water bagels, etc. These are the foods that give you the energy to skate. So take lots of it. Cut out sugary stuff as much as possible. That includes ice cream, candy, cakes and shakes. Yes, I know that's the tasty-to-eat stuff, but they also make you look like an elephant. And elephants don't skate very well! Sugars bring you up and then let you down fast. It is not lasting energy. If you cannot bear to give those ice cream cones up, try this. After a major competition, and only if you win, then go out and stuff your face with all the ice cream you can eat. And take candy for dessert. Just for one day, eat anything and everything. Because tomorrow, you go back to starvation!

The second food to take lots of are proteins. Try chicken and more chicken. If you take enough chicken, you can fly. Actually, the protein from the chicken helps build up those muscles essential for jumping. If you are a vegetarian, then take lots of soybeans which contain tons of proteins too.

The third type of food to take lots of are fruits and vegetables. Eat anything you like from here as long as it does not give you gas. If you feel bloated, then you cannot skate. Furthermore, it smells terrible.

Combine complex carbohydrates with proteins, with fruits and with vegetables. Try chicken linguine, with grapes on the side. Or try chicken and rice, with peaches for dessert. Or try chicken manicotti, with blueberries.

It is essential that you stay away from fats. I don't care what anybody says. Just stay away from them. So anything deep fried in oil, or swimming in milkfat is a definite no. Take away all the skin from the chicken before you eat it. Stay away from anything that even looks suspiciously like fat. It can only harm your skating career.

Plan to eat about three hours prior to competition or general skating. This will give the food plenty of time to digest and settle down. However, don't skate on an empty stomach. Halfway through your program, you will be thinking about how hungry you are instead of the next jump. Furthermore, you will tend to look lethargic or tired on the ice. That does not help your gold medal chances at all!

-14-

Did You Take Your Vitamins Today?

Sometimes, even if you eat like a hippopotamus, you just cannot find the Umph! to perform your best. That is when you have to take some vitamin-mineral supplements.

Since you need some of every type of vitamin/mineral out there, I suggest you buy a bottle of multivitamins/minerals. Brand names really do not matter. Just make sure that the multivitamin/mineral tablets give you one hundred percent of your daily dietary requirements. If you are very rich, then buy the best brand at the most expensive store. If your are not rich, then buy the same bottle at an inexpensive store.

If you feel that you have to take one form of vitamin more than others, then concentrate on the following:

(1) Vitamin B Complex Tablets (Reduce your stress)
(2) Vitamin C Complex (For growth and repair of body)
(3) Vitamin E (Builds up your endurance)

That is it! And do not overdose. That will not help your skating one bit. In fact, it may make you feel worse and/or uncoordinated out there on the ice. And that is not what you want!

-15-

Stretching OR Doing Funny Things On The Floor

You must S-T-R-E-T-C-H before you skate and after you skate. Never mind what other people say, just do it, and you will almost never see injury again. Do not go out there on the ice and start doing triples without this important exercise. You might just as well be committing suicide.

Each stretch that I describe to you here must be held for about 30 seconds or longer. Do them all before you start to skate. I repeat, do them all before you start to skate (and after you skate too). Also, try to do each stretch several times. There is no need to stretch any further when you are on the ice.

Stretch No. 1: Achilles Tendon and Calf Stretch

Assume position as shown. Press heel of back leg to floor. Hold position. Repeat with other leg.

Stretch No. 2: Straddle Stretch

Assume position as shown. Legs should be stretched out as straight as possible perpendicular to body. Now lean forward and touch your chin to the floor. Hold position.

Stretch No. 3: Hurdler's Stretch

Assume position as shown. First, bend forward and touch your forehead to the knee of your outstretched leg. Hold.

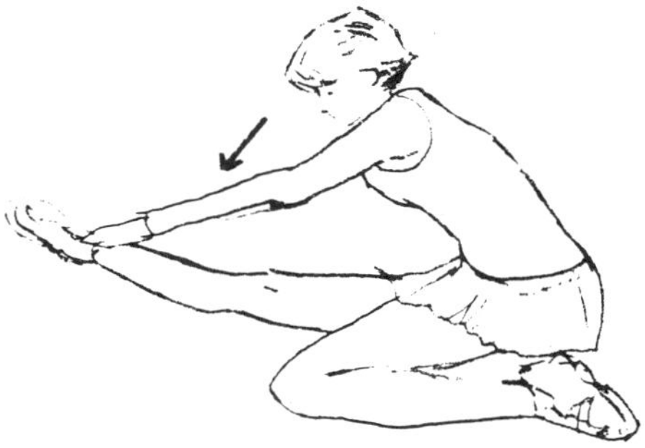

Now lean back, put your elbows on the floor and stretch the other leg. Hold. Repeat with other leg.

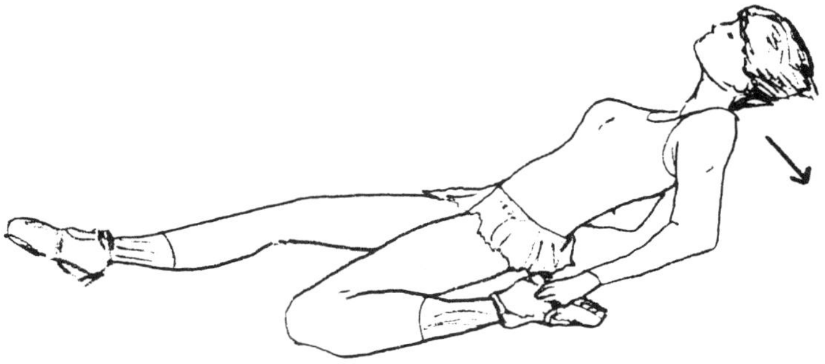

Stretch No. 4: Arm/Shoulder Stretch

Assume position as shown. Put one arm against the corner of a wall or door and then twist your body away from that arm. Hold. Now repeat with other arm.

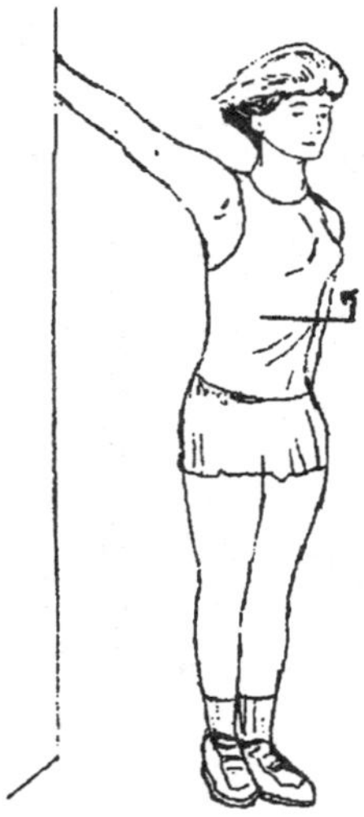

Stretch No. 5: Sitting Stretch

Assume a sitting position as shown. Now, flex toes backwards to knees. Bend forward and stretch arms way beyond your toes. Make sure arms are straight. Hold position.

Stretch No. 6: Back Stretch

First, lie down flat on the floor. Now, do a backward roll such that you lift your legs over your head. Touch toes to floor and chin to chest. Make sure your legs are straight. Hold position.

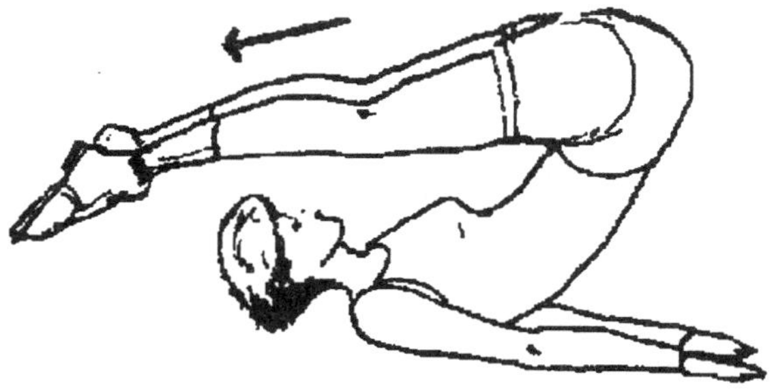

Stretch No. 7: Hip Stretch

Assume position as shown. Make sure arms are bent at chest level. Now rotate your hips (and shoulders) inwards and then backwards forcefully. You can hear your spine "crack" if you listen carefully.

Stretch No. 8: Another Back Stretch

I like to do this back stretch as it gives me a very good layback spin position. Just put your hands on your hips and lean backwards. If you are really good, you can touch your head to your behind.

-16-

Me No Fear

What makes people afraid? People are afraid of things they do not know or do not know very well.

This book will attempt to take away all fears of ice-skating. The mystique of every jump and spin will be taken away. Everything will be explained to you in plain English. You will discover that many of these things are actually very easy!

Once you discover that you cannot really fall down and die out there on the ice (breathe a sigh of relief here), you can go out there and have the time of your life. The whole ice surface is like a big playground. You want to cover as much of it as possible - from end to end and side to side. Even if you fall, you will just end up sliding on the ice. Very, very few figure skaters get hurt on the ice. Figure skating is not hockey. You won't lose teeth or have your body crushed by a mean skating refrigerator disguised as a hockey player.

When you move on to some of the double and triple jumps, admittedly there is a little bit of fear when you first try them out. But if you follow carefully the suggestions given, you can easily beat the fear of doing it. Remember, you need only be afraid if you don't really know how to do it. The moment you know how to do it, then there should be no fear. There would still be a million tries involved before you get up to the triples, but if you persist you will get there. Eventually. If you fear a particular jump or spin, then work on that jump every time you are at the rink. For example, let us say you cannot land that triple Axel but you have all the other triples. My advice to you is to do that triple Axel continuously until you get it. All other triples you can leave out. Never mind if people think you are insane. Never mind if they think you are mad. Never mind if they think you are nuts. Because you know you have to conquer the fear of landing that triple Axel. And you will get it if you are not afraid of it and are willing to take a million falls.

So, as you can see, you don't have to be afraid of anything if you have knowledge of how to do it. And after that, if you are still afraid of something, then you just have to do that thing which you are afraid of until that fear disappears.

-17-

The Secrets Of Jumping Higher

I am now going to describe to you the secrets of jumping higher. If you follow the principles outlined here, you may become the first skater to do a quadruple Axel! And yes, it can be done. It is just very hard to do, that is all.

Secret No 1: Do not break the momentum or flow into the jump. Imagine a pitcher of water spouting from a pipe. Now imagine two pipes through which the water flows. One pipe is bent at a right-angle before the spout like this:

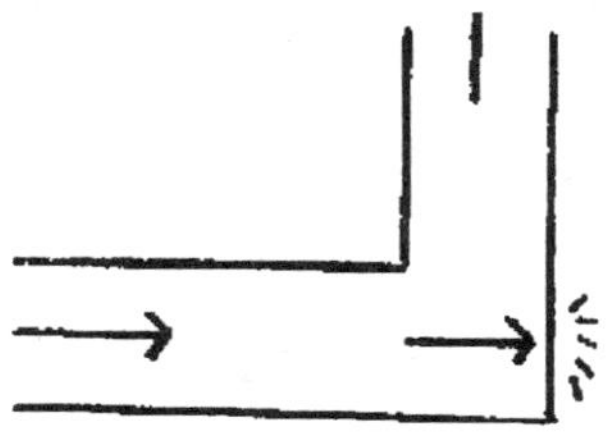

The other pipe is well-rounded or curved before the spout like this:

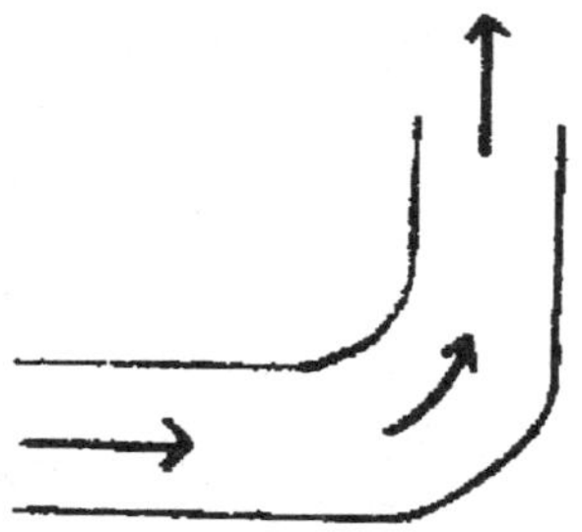

Which pipe do you think will produce the higher spout of water? Of course the well-rounded smooth flowing pipe.

Therefore, before any jump you do, make absolutely sure that you do not come to a complete stop and then try to jump. Otherwise you will never get the height that you are capable of getting. However if you flow right into the jump without hesitation, you can immediately pick up an additional 1-2 feet of vertical height.

Secret No. 2: You must approach any jump with great speed. There is nothing more crucial than this point. I repeat, this is the most important element in producing great, high jumps. I have studied high jumpers clear bars of 7-8 feet up in the air. They can only do that by leading with a very fast run before making the jump. Before you do any jump, do several fast and powerful back or front crossovers to gather speed. As you approach the position for the jump, you must not slow down. If anything, you should accelerate.

I have seen many skaters who can do wonderful single Axels with a fast approach. However, when it came time to do the double Axels, these same skaters will slow down to an almost standstill position before doing the jump. And, of course, they will fall. Why waste energy doing all the crossovers to setup for the jump if you are going to slow down completely before the jump? Don't you want to jump up nice and high? What are you afraid of? If you fall, just get up and do it again. Furthermore, if you are going very fast and you fall, you will just slide on the ice and it really does not hurt at all.

I really don't think too much of coaches who ask their students to jump up, spin three times in the air, and land in the very same spot that they took off from. It is not beautiful and as I said before, you MUST look good on the ice. In addition, if you land close to where you took off, the consistency of landing the jump will be very poor. You must strive for 100% defect-free landings. No excuses.

Secret No. 3: When you are actually jumping, how much vertical height you attain also comes from the upward thrust of your bent free leg and both of your arms. It does not depend entirely on how bent your skating leg is. You must use your free leg and both of your arms to get maximum height.

For example, assume that you are going to do an Axel. As you gather speed (and more speed-Secret No. 2), try putting maximum power into the last crossover before stepping into the position for the jump. Remember, you are going to flow into the jump (Secret No. 1). As you step into your forward edge with your left foot, you do not actually want to bend this left foot too much. Otherwise, you will actually slow down. This will, in turn, make your jump less spectacular. At lift off, the free right leg and both arms should be swung forcefully upwards and around for the spin/spins in the air. The right leg must be bent at the knee. This upward thrust of the free leg is blocked or checked when it reaches hip level. The upward thrust of both arms is blocked or checked when it reaches upper rib cage level. This blocking action actually makes the whole body WEIGHTLESS for a split second. That is the secret why some skaters can jump five feet in the air and why others can only jump five inches. It also gives you the smooth flow into the jump.

To reiterate, you must not slow down or hesitate before any jump. Your speed must not slow down for any reason. The skater who can control his or her body at the fastest speed just before the entrance into the jump will be the highest jumper, all other things equal. You must practice the approach many, many times before you feel comfortable. In fact, most of your practice time must be devoted to controlling high speed. Once you get it, you will almost never lose it.

Remember, too, that jumping is an anti-gravity event. Therefore, if you start to gain weight, make sure that you gain proportional leg strength. Otherwise your improvement will stop. If all your weight is centered around your tummy, then you can join Weight Watchers International.

-18-

What You Put In, You Will Get Out

If you want to become one of the best skaters in the world, you must be prepared to put in the time. In other words, there is a price to pay for it. You have to sacrifice up fattening foods, fattening drinks, wild parties that last for days, etc. You cannot become a part of that life because you have a skating life that demands from you the best you can give.

You must skate for several hours a day minimum, plus off-ice conditioning. If you do not have such time to spare, then skate whenever you can. If you have a choice between a week at the beach or a week of ice-time, then you choose the ice-time. It requires sacrifice. I know that it is very hard, but if you want to become the best you must be prepared to sacrifice up many things.

If you put in only an hour of skating a week, do not expect to get very good. You will never get that triple jump if you spend only one hour on the ice per week. There may be some of you out there who think that you can get a triple Axel if you skate one hour a week. If you are one of those, then you must be crazy. It cannot be done. You belong to the insane asylum, not on the ice-rink. Every good skater has spent thousands of hours on and off the ice, training and training until they finally become excellent. Did you get that? You must spend thousands and thousands of hours in training before you can become the best. In other words, what you put in, that is what you will get out. Are you prepared to give that sort of sacrifice?

-19-

Terms Which You Must Know

Terms	**What It Means**
1. Skating Foot	The foot that you are skating (standing) on.
2. Free Foot	The foot that you are not skating (standing) on.
3. Inside Edge	Edge which is good and still inside. Actually, it is that edge which is where the arch of your foot is.
4. Outside Edge	Edge which is bad and has been sent outside.
5. Flat	Not inside or outside.
6. Single Jumps	Jumps which are supposed to have 1 revolution (but don't believe it).
7. Double Jumps	Jumps which are 10 times harder than the single jumps.
8. Triple Jumps	Jumps which win you the gold medal.
9. Coaches	Those people who make big bucks.
10. Skating Rink	Where you spend part of your life.
11. Zamboni	Some cute, Italian guy.
12. Free Skating Ice Time	The most expensive thing you can buy.
13. Mothers	The nicest people in this world.
14. Fathers	The poorest people in this world. (Look at those $800 skates!)
15. Death Drop	Help! I've fallen and I can't get up!
16. Working-Out	Personal torture.
17. Plyometrics	Say what?
18. Fast Spins	Invented to make you throw up.
19. Biellman Spin	The spin which killed me.
20. Winner	The person who has tried his/her best.
21. Loser	The person who did not try.
22. Smart	The people who bought this book!
23. Cars	Where you spend the rest of your life.
24. Beautiful	That is YOU!

-20-

What?! You Have Never Been On The Ice Before?

Are you an absolute beginner? Then read this. Just put on your ice-skates and go out there on the ice. Grab the wall. Grab your friends. Grab anything. Never mind if you look terrible and terrified. Never mind if you fall and stand on your head. Never mind if your brain leaves you. Never mind if your legs and your head start fighting. Never mind if your ankles are screaming at you, "Are you crazy? You expect us, your ankles, to do this?" Never mind all of that - just go out there and do it.

The main thing that you have to know right now is that you must get over the initial fear of being on the ice! And the only way to get over that fear is to get out there and do it. That is the only way. When I first stepped on the ice many years ago, I took only one step on the ice, clung to the boards, came back in took off my ice-skates, and left the ice-rink. I was terrified! But I came back the next day...

So, just go out there and do it. And as the years pass, a champion will take the place of that terrified person. It always begins with that first step, that first try, that first push, ...

-21-

For Beginners Only

Now that you have gotten around the rink a few times, it is time to make you into somebody. Follow these instructions carefully.

Trick No. 1: Gliding on Two Feet Going Forward

Skate around anyway you like. Gather a little speed. Now place both your feet together and stand up straight. You will begin to glide.

Trick No. 2: Gliding on One Foot Going Forward

Begin by gliding on two feet. Now lift your right foot straight up by bending your right knee. Make sure there is no gap between your legs. All your weight is now on the left foot. Glide on this left foot. Now repeat with the other foot.

Trick No. 3: Gliding with One Foot Pointing Forwards

Begin by gliding on one foot. Now push your free foot out in front of you. Make sure that the toe is pointed down diagonally in front of you. The inside edge is facing upwards, towards the ceiling. Glide for as long as you can. The legs must be straight. Now do it with the other foot.

Trick No. 4: Glide with One Foot Pointing Backwards

Begin by gliding on one foot. Now push your free foot straight behind you. The toe is pointed down diagonally backwards. The outside edge is facing upwards towards the ceiling. Glide forever. Once again, the legs must be straight. Now do it with the other foot.

Trick No. 5: Gliding, Full-Squat Position

Begin by gliding on both feet. Now, go down immediately into a full-squat position. Make sure you are down completely and that your feet are together. You must go down completely because of the sit-spin position that you will learn later. When you are down all the way, your behind is just a couple of inches above the ice and your hamstrings are touching your calf muscles. Push your arms out in front of you to balance yourself.

Trick No. 6: Stopping

Forget about other stops and just do this one. Stand up straight. Put your left arm in front of you and your right arm behind your. Put your right foot in a T-position behind your left foot as shown. Push off gently with your right foot. Glide on left foot. Now close back your right foot to your left foot by shaving the ice with your right foot. Make sure the right foot "sticks" to the left foot as you do this. There must be no gap between the feet. Bend the right knee a little bit. When you get better, lean backwards as you are stopping so you can use the right outside edge to stop.

Trick No. 7: Going Backwards

There is no need to learn how to go backwards right now. All beginning methods of going backwards are ugly, so you can forget them until the next chapter when I will teach you the back crossovers.

-22-

Are You A Lefty?

Hi, Lefties! Sorry, but all the jumps and spins described here in this book are for righties. But you can easily switch left to right and right to left, can't you? Once again, I apologize for this inconvenience. Just switch the direction of everything I say around and you will be okay.

Remember, it is not whether you are left-handed or right-handed that makes you a champion. What makes you a champion is what you have inside of you.

-23-

In The Beginning, There Was The Edge

This is the most important chapter in this book, so pay special attention to this chapter. You may have skated for 10 years, but you may still not have good edges. This chapter will cover all basic stroking right to the three-turns. Every time you are at the rink, you must do all the items described here. It does not matter whether you are a beginner or an Olympic medalist skater, you must have good edges. Otherwise, you will not look good on the ice. You must skate with good, clean, sharp edges starting right now or you will never look good. That is a guarantee.

Basic Forward Stroking

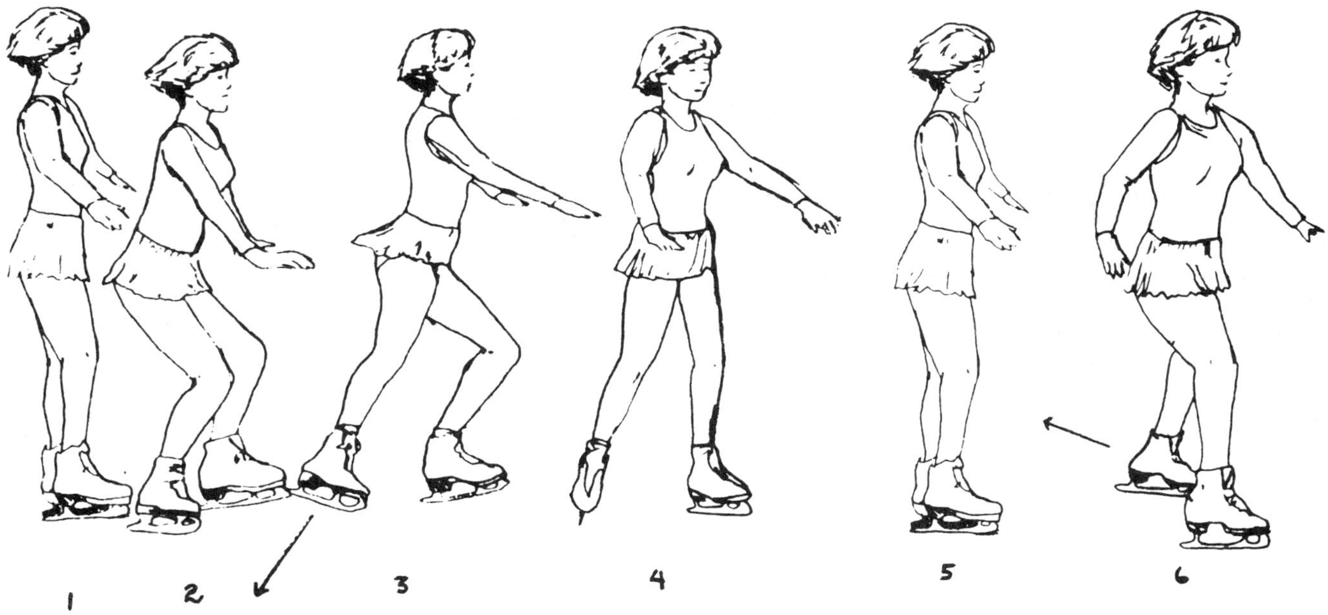

Keep your head straight and your back arched as you do this.

1. Stand straight. Arms to side at rib-cage level. Legs straight.
2. Push to the side (not backwards) with your right foot. Use your whole blade, not the toe pick.
3. Transfer all weight to left foot. Bend left foot deeply.
4. Glide on left foot.
5. Close back right foot to left foot. Touch boots together.
6. Push off with left foot now. Use whole skate. Push to the side, not backwards.
7. Transfer all weight to deeply bent right foot and glide. Note that arms do not move at all when you are stroking.

Forward Inside Edge

1. Stand straight in T-position. Left arm in front. Right arm behind. Push forward onto left inside edge with right foot. After the push, bring back the right foot and touch it to the left foot as shown. No gap between the legs, please. Arms do not move from original position. Let the blade do all the work. You just stand on it.
2. Do a complete half-circle on the ice on that inside edge. Do not move your arms at all. Keep your body straight.
3. Now do the exact same thing using the other foot. You will be doing the right inside edge. Your right arm is in front and your left arm is behind you now.

Forward Outside Edge

1. Stand straight in T-position. Left arm in front. Right arm behind. Push forward onto left outside edge with right foot. After the push, bring back the right foot and touch it to the left foot. No gap between legs again. Arms stay where they are. Keep your body straight throughout.
2. Do a complete half-circle on that left leg. Let the blade do the outside edge. You just stand on that blade.
3. Now do it with the other foot. You will be doing the right outside edge. Your right arm is in front and your left arm is behind you.

Backward Outside Edge

1. Stand perpendicular to the half-circle which you will be going on. Your left arm is in front and your right arm is behind you.
2. Push off forward diagonally with your left foot and stand on right back outside edge simultaneously. Make sure your right knee is bent. Look backward.
3. Stand up straight now and let the blade do the work. The blade will do a half-circle. All you do is stand on it and do not move your arms. Put your feet close together. Continue looking backwards.
4. Repeat with other leg. Your right arm is in front and your left arm is behind you.

Backward Inside Edge

1. Stand straight. Your left arm is in front and your right arm is behind you. Now push off with left foot forward. At the same time, turn the right foot and step onto the back inside edge. You must turn the right foot to catch this elusive edge. Bend that right knee, too.
2. Now stand up straight on that right leg. Keep your legs close together. Do not move your arms. Let the blade do the work. Look backwards over your right shoulder. You should be able to do a half circle.
3. Now do it with the other foot. Your right arm is in front and your left arm is behind you.

Forward Three Turn

1. Stand straight in T-position. Your right arm is in front and your left arm is behind you. Push off with left foot and do the forward outside edge on your right foot. Bend this right knee deeply.
2. Suddenly straighten up the right knee and turn your hips as shown. Your whole blade will turn from forwards to backwards. You must be quick on the turn. Remember, turn the hips. You do not turn your shoulders or arms.
3. After the turn, bend your right knee deeply again and ride out that back inside edge. Your shoulders and arms do not move at all from start to finish.
4. Repeat with other foot. Your left arm is in front and your right arm is behind you.

Forward Crossovers

Skate in a circle to practice this. Do this every time you are on the ice.

1. Push off to the side with right foot.
2. Glide on bent left foot (forward outside edge). Right foot should be straight out to the side. Glide.
3. Begin to bring right foot forward and cross it over the left foot. Bend this right knee deeply while doing this. You are skating with both feet now.
4. Now push off behind with left foot. You are now skating on your right foot inside edge.
5. Bring left foot back now and touch it to right foot before pushing off with right foot again. Repeat.
6. Now do it going in the other direction. Your left arm is in front and your right arm is behind you.

Backward Crossovers

This is your first lesson on going backwards. Do this on a circle. When you do the back crossover well, it is the most powerful movement you can have on the ice. You can ultimately travel across the ice at 40 miles per hour. There is no other stroking or crossover move more powerful than this. Just remember to bend both legs while doing this crossover. Do backward crossovers every time you are on the ice.

1. Stand up straight. Your right arm is behind you and your left arm is in front. Do not move your arms from this position. Look backwards down your right arm.
2. Slide your left foot over your right foot using your back left inside edge. Bend this left foot deeply. You do not lift the left foot off the ice.
3. Push the right foot diagonally back. Make sure it is straight. All your weight is on your left foot. Glide on this left backward inside edge.
4. Bring the right foot back now and reach far into the circle. The two feet must be far apart from one another. This gives you power. Make sure your right knee is deeply bent. Your weight is on your right foot.
5. Now slide that bent left foot over the right foot again. At the same time, push back diagonally with that right foot. Now your weight is on your left foot.
6. Now go in the other direction. Your right arm is in front of you and your left arm is behind you.

-24-

The Secret To Doing The Singles

Every single jump must be approached with the greatest amount of speed possible. You must never do singles at slow speeds. Every single jump should cover as much ice as possible. Think about taking up the whole rink before landing any single jump. If you can do all single jumps at great speed, it will greatly help you when you move on to your doubles and triples. This is the first secret.

The second secret is that your body must be as straight as possible BEFORE you take off from the ice. Try your best not to lean forward too much, especially for the Flip and the Lutz. If you start leaning too far forward now, you will lean more when you move on to your doubles/triples and completely mess up the rotations in the air.

The third secret is that you must concentrate on jumping up straight in the air. This is the only way to make sure that you stay straight when you are in the air. This is of number one importance. Without a straight body, you can forget about going for the Olympics. You must jump up straight so that you can be straight in the air. There must be no bend of the body in the air at all. And there are no exceptions to this absolute rule. You must be straight in the air. Period.

The fourth secret is that you must cross your left foot over your right foot for all your jumps. Never ever leave the left foot hanging at the side. You will never be able to do some of the harder jumps later on. No matter how easy the jump is, cross your left foot over your right foot when you are in the air.

The fifth secret is to "land softly" on your right foot. Think about landing without any noise. Think about landing on tiptoes. Make as little noise as possible on your landings. The only way to do that is to land on your toe-picks and bend the right knee deeply to absorb the shock of the landing. If you remember this, your landings will always be consistent.

To summarize:

1. Skate with great speed.
2. Make sure your body is as straight as possible before takeoff.
3. Make sure your body is absolutely straight in the air.
4. Cross your left foot over your right foot in the air.
5. Land softly, by bending your right foot deeply on landing.

-25-

The Single Jumps

The single jumps are very easy. Make sure you follow everything I describe here carefully. When I say straight, I mean straight. When I say bent, I mean bent. When I say stretch, I mean stretch. If you do this, you can get all the single jumps in a very, very short time.

Make sure that all jumps are done in a STRAIGHT LINE. That means that all jumps must cover many feet across the ice in a straight line. There are many theories on this but none had worked for me until I jumped in a straight line, covering a minimum of 3 feet across the ice to about 11 feet. You must jump in a straight line, because that gives you time to "hang" in the air and do the triples later on. If you do not have that "hang-time" in the air, you cannot do the triples later on.

The jumps that I want you to do here will prepare you for the more advanced jumps later on. I do not want you to learn something that has no value later on-like a bunny hop. That is because you will never use that jump later on. My theory is: Why learn anything which you will NEVER use or put into competition? You should rather put all your time into mastering, say the Axel. That is also why all half-jumps are left out here. Why do half-jumps when you are supposed to do the whole jump? If you fall, just get up and do it again. And again. And again.

Always practice doing the jump itself - not something that resembles it. For example, when doing the Axel, do the Axel - not a Watz jump and then a Loop. You can NEVER get the Axel that way. Just do the Axel - that is the only way to get it. And you will get it much faster, too.

(Yes! You are right. This is a blank page.)

The Waltz Jump

1. Do backward crossovers, gather great speed, and stand on your back outside edge of your right foot. Keep your left foot close to your right foot. Keep your body straight. Step forward onto your left outside edge.
2. You must be on an outside edge. Bend this left leg. Just ride on this edge. Do NOT jump yet. Stretch your right foot and both arms backward. Make sure your chin is up. Do not look down at the ice.
3. Now, throw your right leg and arms straight through in a straight line. Try to cover at least 10 feet across the ice. You jump off your left toe-pick. Jump in a straight line. Just jump straight out in a straight line going forward.

4. If you have thrown your right foot straight through, you will achieve the beautiful split position in the air. You must try to hang in the air for about 1-2 seconds to get used to staying in the air.
5. Now land on your right toe pick going backward on the back outside edge. Bend your right leg deeply both to absorb the shock of landing and to glide backward.
6. Glide away on this back outside edge. Count 1-5 slowly as you glide backward. Your arms are to the side and your left leg is pointing straight out diagonally to the side and back. Make sure your chin is up. Make this beautiful.

The Salchow Jump

1. Do backward crossovers, gather great speed, and stand on your right back outside edge on your right foot. Keep your body straight.
2. Step forward on your left outside edge to do a three-turn. Put your left arm in front and your right arm behind you.
3. Do the three-turn here.
4. You are now going backward on your left inside edge. HOLD THIS POSITION. Do not jump yet. You must hold this inside edge. You do not bend your left knee too much. Think about going backward in a straight line on your back inside edge. Do this by pushing your left arm straight out firmly.

7

5. Now start the swing around of the right foot and right arm. Keep this right foot as far away from the left foot as possible. You are still standing straight on your left foot. Do not bend this left foot yet. As the right foot swings around more begin to bend the left foot in preparation for the jump.
6. When you have swung completely around and are looking forward, jump up from the toe-pick and project yourself forward, just like in the Waltz jump. Make sure that you jump only when you are facing forward. Make doubly sure you are jumping in a straight line, otherwise you can never do the triple Salchow later on.
7. Land as usual. Count 1-5 as you glide away.

The Loop Jump

1. Do a forward three-turn on your left leg. Your left arm is in front and your right arm is behind you.
2. Step on your right back outside edge. Keep the left foot in front and a little bit to the side of the right foot on the inside edge. You are on both feet. Just stand up straight on both legs. Look straight ahead.
3. As you are about to jump, bend your right knee deeply and do a deep right outside edge. Your left leg must still be in front and a little bit to the side of your right leg. Keep your arms low so that you can whip them around and up when you jump. Make sure your right arm is firmly pressed back. Make sure all your weight is on your right hip. Make sure you are going backward in a straight line.

4. As the right backward edge gets the deepest, turn around forward fast and jump off from the toe pick. Remember, do not jump until your are facing forward. The right arm swings upward and around forcefully. You must use this right arm. You must jump facing forward, otherwise you cannot do the triple loop later on. Bend the left knee and cross the left foot across the right foot. These two feet must touch each other as you spin in the air. Remember, they must touch each other. You must also remember to jump in a straight line.
5. Land, as usual.

The Flip Jump

1. Glide on left leg going forward with right foot straight in front. Stand straight.
2. Do a three-turn on your left foot outside edge. Use your right foot toe-pick to push into your three-turn.
3. You are now going backward on a shallow left inside edge. Your left knee is bent deeply. Make sure you are going backward in a straight line. Your right arm is pushed way behind you. Hold for a split second. Do not bend forward too much. Keep your body as arched as possible.

4. Reach back straight with your right toe-pick and dig that toe-pick into the ice lightly. The moment your toe-pick digs in the ice, start turning around forcefully and shift all your weight onto that toe-pick. You do this by straightening your left foot and transferring all your weight from the left foot to the right toe-pick. Remember, you are flying backward in a straight line. You turn around forcefully by violently swinging that right arm and shoulder around and up at the same time. You also swing the left arm back.
5. Jump up only when your are facing forward. Keep your feet crossed lightly. They must be tightly crossed.
6. Land, as usual.

The Lutz Jump

Do this jump moving toward the corners of the ice-rink. However, try to do this jump way before you hit the boards.

1. Do backward crossovers, gather great speed, and stand up straight on your left leg going backward. You are going backward fast toward the corner, just standing on your left foot. Your left arm is in front and your right arm is behind you.
2. Suddenly bend deeply on your left knee and curve into a back outside edge. At the same time, reach straight back with your right toe-pick and pick lightly into the ice. Do not bend too far forward. Reach forward with your left arm and reach backward with your right arm.

3. The moment your right toe-pick digs into the ice, swing your right arm and shoulder violently up and around, and jump upward from your right toe-pick. You must be facing forward as you leave the ice. You are flying backward as you are spinning. Make sure you jump backward in a straight line - straight toward the corner of the rink. Cross your legs tightly together. You must cross your legs together.
4. Land, as usual.

The Axel Jump

This is the highest and longest jump you can ever do on the ice. When done well, you can feel what "flying" is like. No triple jump can ever be that high or that long.

1. Do backward crossovers, gather great speed, and stand on your back outside edge on your right foot. Keep your body straight.
2. Step forward on a left outside edge. Make sure this edge is deep. Stretch both arms back. Your right knee is bent deeply behind you. Make sure your chin is up. You are leaning very slightly forward during take-off. The take-off is from the left toe-pick.
3. Jump up and spin around at the SAME time in a straight line. You must be spinning as you are climbing upward. Use your right shoulder, right hip and right knee to spin your body around. Your right knee is deeply bent as you swing it up and around. You must be perfectly straight on your right side when jumping. DO NOT jump up and then try to spin. There will be no spin if you are not already spinning as you are climbing up. You must be spinning as you are climbing up. That is essential for quick, multiple revolutions in the air. Remember, you are jumping in a

straight line, so your landing must be about 10 feet in front of you. You do not jump around. Jump in a straight line. You spin around, not jump around. Think right hip, right shoulder all the time so you can be straight in the air on your right side. Your left leg must be crossed around your right leg tightly. Do not put it to the side, otherwise you will NEVER get the double Axel later on. Your arms must also be wrapped tightly to your chest. Also, as you are jumping up, turn your head to the left to assist you in the revolutions. You must be aggressive in this jump. It is like a do-it-or-die thing. Once again, you must spin as you are jumping up, and your landing must be 10 feet directly in front of you. You must, must, must jump in a straight line, otherwise this jump will be impossible.

4. Land, as usual.

The Single Toe Loop

I like to do the toe loops only as combination jumps, after landing from the Axels or Lutzes. If you learn it this way, you will automatically take off after landing from the first jump. The single toe loop is very easy.

1. Land after an Axel or Lutz jump, with the left arm in front. Keep your body straight. Reach back straight with your left toe pick and tap into the ice.

2. Immediately, swing the right arm and shoulder around forcefully and take off facing forward. You jump up with your right leg. Do a waltz jump and land as usual. Jump in a straight line backward.
3. Land.

-26-

Are You Dead Out There On The Ice?

When you are out there on the ice, please show some enthusiasm. Don't look like a dead rat out there going through certain motions. No dead rat has ever won any major competitions. Dead rats never win anything. That is because they are DEAD.

Show the audience that you are alive and kicking. Your whole posture should shout, "I am alive. Look at me!"

Let us start with your head. Are you looking down at the ice all the time? There's nobody in the ice. Why are you looking down there? Look up and smile widely at the audience. Those are the people you should be looking at. Thrust your chin up. Grin at the cameras. Always keep your head up and smile widely.

Now take a look at your hands. Are they down by your side? Are you a skating Frankenstein monster? Are you sleep-skating? Use your hands. Lift them up to heaven. Point them at the audience. Open up your arms to embrace them. Stretch them out all the time. You can even put your hand on your hips and strike up an attitude. Do anything. Just don't put those hands down limply by your side.

Now take a look at your back. Are you all hunched up? Are you playing the Hunchback of the Skating Rink? If not, then arch that back. Everything you do will look better with an arched back. When you land from a jump, arch that back. When you spin, arch that back. When you glide, arch that back.

The most horrible-to-watch skater is the one who looks dead on the ice. If you have to take one pound of sugar to make you alive, then take that one pound of sugar. Or take ten Snickers' bars. Do whatever it takes to become alive. Have a spark out there. Be sparky. Be clever. Be naughty. Be spunky. Be carefree. Be graceful. Be anything. Just don't be dead.

-27-

What? Are You Still Thinking About That?

As you read through this book and gain confidence, sometimes that thing happens and you stop progressing. "That thing" is your past skating history. For example, you unconsciously tell yourself that you can never do the Axel because you have tried it for years and could never do it.

Now I am going to tell you a big secret. If you are going to let past failures influence your future, then you should stop skating immediately. Why? Because you are not going to succeed. You must let go of the past and reach forward to the future. Always reach forward, never backward.

If you have failed one million times before on that jump, it just means that you are one million times closer to getting it. Maybe the one millionth and one time! Some jumps and spins look impossible, but they actually are just hard - not impossible. Relearn the techniques and try again. Once again, your past must not influence your future success.

Your past is over and done with. Why worry about it? Toss it out. Make the decision today to become the best skater you can possibly be. That may take a lot of tomorrows, but that is what you have - all the tomorrows in the world. And one day you will get that jump, that spin, that footwork, that style, etc. So set your sights onward and do not look backward. Only then can you skate perfectly.

-28-

Why Are You Doing This?

From time to time, you may lose interest in skating for a while. This happens because it gets hard, or you just do not know what you are doing with your skating life.

This is the time when you have to sit back and ask yourself, "What are my skating objectives?" The moment you lose sight of your objectives, then you will lose heart in skating. Ask yourself what your objectives are.

If your skating objective is just to have fun, then maybe you are working at it too hard. Slow down and put the fun back. Or skate with a partner. That always is fun.

If your skating objective is to reach Olympic level, then tell yourself everyday that this is your objective. This will help you continue on. This will make you get up when you splatter on the ice. This will bring you to the rink on those -40°F days. This will help you jump up higher when you do not feel like jumping at all. That objective will serve as your light which will guide you onward.

If your skating objective is to be the best you can be, then maybe you lost heart in skating because you have reached the best you can be at that level. Now is the time to set new and higher objectives. This gives you reason to move on. Otherwise, you are just stuck at a level. Set new goals and move forward again.

If your skating objective is to please somebody else, then you must rethink your whole skating life. Why should you skate to please somebody else? That will always lead to frustration because you do not like it yourself. You must like skating yourself. You do not skate for somebody else. Otherwise, you are just deceiving yourself. Maybe you should sit down and reexamine everything. Maybe you will be happiest doing something else. Remember, not skating is not the end of the world.

-29-

The Secret To Doing Doubles And Triples

Before you start doing multiple revolutions in the air, make sure that you have some muscles. Turn back to the chapter on working out and develop your leg and arm muscles. It is impossible to do a triple Axel without strength. It is impossible to do a double Axel without strength, also.

The first secret is to try to approach all the doubles/triples/quads with as much speed as possible. I said try, because you will actually slow down a bit - because you are preparing to spin more times in the air. You are preparing to explode in the air. However, there are no excuses for losing speed altogether. So try to approach the jumps with as much speed as possible.

The second secret is that your body has to be straighter (than the singles) before take off. This will greatly help you jump up straight. I try to look at the audience and arch my back at the same time to be straight before takeoff. This will make sure that my head is looking up and my back is not leaning over.

The third secret is the biggest secret of all. You must be prepared to spin the doubles/triples/quads while still on the ice! You jump up straight while spinning. You must be already spinning while jumping up. This goes together. You cannot do the triples if you jump up first and then try to spin while up there in the air. It cannot be done. I wasted years trying this. It just cannot be done. You must already be spinning when you jump up straight. That is why most jumps are a little "cheated" - because you spin the first half while jumping up. I always think of it as a "very violent spin up there in the air." I swing my left and right arm around violently while I am jumping up straight in the air. If I don't think a "very violent spin," I just cannot complete up the revolutions. To me, my right arm is swinging around violently and upward as well. I make sure that I am straight in the air by concentration on my right hip and making sure that there is no bend in my right hip at all. You may be surprised, but you can easily do doubles and triples with this technique. However, there will be less height because you are spinning as you are jumping up.

The fourth secret is that you must fold in your arms and cross your legs as fast as possible. You cannot afford to wait even a split second. I wasted years trying to jump up first, waiting half-a-second, and then crossing. It does not work. You cross as you are taking off violently. Sometimes I manage to thump myself across the chest as I fold in my arms, or kick my shin bone with my crossing leg. But that's okay. Think about making yourself as straight and as small as possible. Do not leave your armpits open too much while doing the triples. It slows you down and leaves a bad smell as well. Keep them as close to your body as possible. Your legs must be straight, with your thighs closed while in the cross position in the air. Therefore, you must start folding as you are taking off from the ice and then you fold in really tight while you are in the air. If you can do this, you have your triples. Make sure you keep your armpits closed and make sure your legs are straight while in the air.

-30-

The Double Jumps

The jumps now get hard. You can get all the single jumps in about two months, but the doubles may take you 6-9 months - especially the double Axel. But once you get the doubles, you will find out that they are no big deal either.

You must have continued working out and maintaining a disciplined nutrition plan. Do lots of doubles off-ice first before attempting to do them on the ice. Make sure your body is straight in the air when doing the doubles off-ice. If you are not straight off-ice, you will not be straight on-ice. The purpose in doing all these jumps off-ice first is to get used to the quick, fast revolutions needed to complete up the jumps. What you are doing is training the right and left shoulder to rotate rapidly around together with your hips in the air, looking over your left shoulder. Once you get used to the position, it is quite easy to transfer it to the ice. I find that the doubles come easy once you develop some upper body strength. The reason is that the arms and shoulders can swing around more forcefully, propelling the body rapidly around in a fast, tight spin. When you have less upper body strength, you may not be able to force yourself to spin around that fast.

A disciplined nutrition plan is essential, because this is no time to be putting on weight without substantial muscle gain. Remember, you are jumping up and spinning around at the same time. Getting too fat is not helpful here. You do not need to be very smart to figure out that it is harder for an elephant to do a double Axel than a thin monkey.

Enough talk, now let us begin the doubles.

The Double Salchow

This is an easy double, as it actually is just an Axel at the end of a three-turn. Try to do this double first.

1. Enter the jump exactly like the single Salchow.
2. Make sure you hold this back inside edge, and do not lean forward too much. I can hold this back inside edge for half the rink's length.
3. I try to be completely straight here just before the jump.

4. Make sure you are facing forward when you do the Axel here. Remember to jump in a straight line. You should land about 5 feet in a straight line in front of where you took off. Do not be afraid to jump in a straight line.
5. Land, as usual.

The Double Loop

I like to do this double jump next.

1. Enter the jump exactly the same, like the single loop.
2. Take a deeper outside edge on your right foot before the jump. Make sure your left foot is in front of your right foot. Make sure that your arms are firmly checked so that you can explode them up and around at the SAME TIME. Either you are prepared to explode forcefully enough to do the double, or you are not.
3. Explode and jump up facing forward. The moment you jump up, you are spinning. The double is either here or it is not here at this point. If your arms and shoulders did not swing up and around violently enough, you cannot get the double. If your legs are not crossed tightly here, you cannot get the double. If your body is not straight here, you will fall. Make absolutely sure that your shoulders are at the same level. Your right shoulder must not be lower than your left shoulder. This is why

you must explode your right arm and shoulder up and around. If you do not punch it up forcefully, your left shoulder will be higher and you will not be straight in the air. And then you will fall when you land. That is a guarantee. Also, make sure that you are looking to the left when exploding up and around. If everything is right, the double is already finished here.

4. While you are spinning in the air, you will see nothing because everything is over in less than one second. Like I said, the double already happened when you jumped up and around. You cannot start the spin here. The spin already took place during the right back outside edge and the explosion upward and around.
5. Land, as usual about 4 feet from your toe-pick takeoff point.

The Double Flip

1. Enter the jump just like the single Flip.
2. Make sure that your body is not leaning too far forward. It is very hard to do the double if you are leaning way forward. Remember you are flying backward from your left foot to your right toe-pick. When you jump, all your weight is on your right side. Remember, you are jumping in a straight line going backward. But you face forward for the take off. All this happens in a split second.

3. The moment I take off, I just think of a double Loop and do everything the same as in a double Loop. At this point, the double is already there or it is not.
4. You do not do the double here. It is already over with if it wasn't there before at Step 3.
5. Land, as usual - about 5 feet from when you picked in the ice.

The Double Lutz

For many people, this is an easy jump. It is one of my favorites.

1. Enter the jump just like in the single Lutz.
2. Bend the left knee deeply just before the toe-pick dig-in by the right foot. Try also not to lean forward too much.

3. The jump actually happens here when you are swinging your arms and body around. If you are not exploding fast enough, you cannot get the double Lutz.
4. Make sure you travel in a straight line going backward.
5. Land, as usual - about 7 feet from where your toe-picks dug into the ice.

The Double Axel

This is the jump which makes many people give up skating for good. But it is really not that difficult if you follow some advice here. This jump is not as high as the single Axel. That is because you have to spin more at take-off. Therefore, you sacrifice up some height.

1. Enter the jump just like in the single Axel.
2. Make absolutely sure that you step into a deep, big edge. Try to hold this position a while before the actual jump. Because you have to spin more forcefully while taking off, you will see a skid mark on the ice after the toe-pick. The skid mark tells you that you are spinning around as you are climbing up.

3. You must be spinning violently around as you are climbing upward. There is no other way to do this jump. You MUST also jump out in a straight line. If you jump around, instead of out, I guarantee you that you will fall. Try to squeeze the air out of your armpits while you are spinning. That gives you a tighter spin. Make absolutely sure that your shoulders and body are perfectly straight in the air.
4. Make sure your legs are straight when spinning in the air. The left knee must not be bent. Think about squeezing a grasshopper between your thighs.
5. Land, as usual.

The Double Toe Loop

Once again, do the double Toe after landing from a double Axel or a double Lutz. The double Toe is very easy if you can spin around and take-off facing forward. You do not travel backward very far in the toe loop jumps.

1. Land from a double Axel, and then reach back with your left toe pick to tap into the ice. Tap straight back. Do not ever tap the ice on your right foot side of the ice. You have to bend the right knee so that you can jump up.

2. Immediately, start to spin around forcefully with your right arm and shoulder. Jump up with your right foot (when facing forward) and immediately cross your left foot over your right foot facing forward as you are jumping upward. Make absolutely sure that your shoulders and hips spin around at the same time. If you spin your shoulders around first before your hips, you will bend at the hips and lean over when you land from the jump.
3. Close the left leg straight over your right leg as you spin. Do not bend the left leg at the knee.

-31-

How To Be Naughty Before An Audience

Unless you are a seasoned professional skater, there is always the fear of skating before an audience. This fear is perfectly natural. It comes from being afraid of making a complete fool of yourself in front of so many people. You are afraid of crashing onto the ice and spilling your brains and guts out on the ice. You are afraid that you are not good enough. You are afraid that you do not look graceful enough. So, what do you do?

I used one secret for many years. What you do is you pick out one person in the audience (maybe your skating friend) and then you skate for that one person. Try to blank out everybody else. Never mind about the cameras. Never mind about the judges. Never mind about all the other people. Skate for that one person. However, make sure that you know where that person is sitting beforehand. Ask her/him to wear a bright red sweater or something like that. That helps you spot her/him. You will find that there is minimal tension if you are skating for that friend of yours. After all, she/he has probably seen you mess up a million times before. So what's new if you mess up again? What's the big deal if you cannot land that triple jump? Your friend has seen that a million times before. In fact, it was just yesterday when you failed to land that triple. See, that should get you relaxed. It really is no big deal.

You will also find it easier to smile if you concentrate on that one person. It is hard to smile for everybody. But it is easy to smile for just one person.

Remember, blank out everybody else and concentrate on that one person. It works wonders in relaxing you. And when you are relaxed, you can be as naughty as you want to be!

-32-

This One Thing I Do

If you have difficulty landing some jumps or doing some spins, maybe it is because you are trying to learn too many new things all at once. If you do too many new things at once, you may not perfect anything. In fact, you may get frustrated because nothing seems to be working. What you have to do is try to do only one thing at a time. That way you can concentrate all your efforts on that one item. Get it reasonably well, then move on to the next item.

For example, if you are still falling from your double Axel, then do not attempt too many triple Toes. That is because you may not be fast and tight enough on your spins in the air for the double Axel. If you do the triple Toe simultaneously, you are almost guaranteed to fall. Try to perfect the double Axel first, then move on to the triple Toe. Otherwise, you have two things to worry about. And you do not need to have more worries. You have enough already.

Another example would be in a spin (spins are described later). If you still cannot center a fast scratch spin, then do not do a fast layback spin. It just cannot be done. The laybacks require a nice center before you can actually lay back. Work and work on that scratch spin until you perfect it, then you can learn the next five spins in one day. So once again, try to learn one new thing at a time. Do not do everything new at once, otherwise it will just lead to frustration. You will find yourself progressing much faster if you just do one thing at a time.

-33-

Where Is Your Brain?

While you are setting up for any jump, your whole mind must be concentrating on the jump. You could be looking at the audience but you will not see them because you are focusing inward. This is extremely important, because the moment your focus is on some other thing, you will start to mess up. You will lose speed, lose the aggressiveness when you take off and then you will fall. Why? Because you will not be able to complete up those multiple revolutions in the air.

Do not get distracted by anything or anybody. Even if you have landed every triple in your program and are now preparing for the easiest jump in your short program, say a double Axel, you must concentrate fully on it. One moment of non-concentration and you will fall - even if you have landed that jump a million times before. Never let your guard down until the program is finished. I repeat, never lose your concentration and let your guard down until your program is finished.

-34-
Do It A Badzillion Times

I am a firm believer in repetitions until you get the jump or spin. This principle is most important when you are learning a new jump. Once you have the technique down pat, then you just do that jump a million times until you get it. Note that you must know the correct technique first before beginning the repetitions. If you practice an incorrect technique and then do it repetitiously, then you will just learn a bad habit. That is the craziest thing you can do.

So, once you know the correct technique, then just practice that jump or spin until you get it. No matter how sick you get of that jump/spin, you must just keep doing it until you get it. Even if you vomit, you just clean your mouth and do it again. Do it until you get it.

Also, repeat the jump or spin in the same spot all the time. For example, if you pick the two corners of the ice rink to do your triple Lutzes, then just do it in those two corners. Don't show off and do it in the middle of the rink. Do the jumps/spins in the same spot each time. This method tends to eliminate fears and improve consistency in landings.

-35-

Do It OR Die Trying

Okay, so you cannot do something. Is that why you are frustrated? Is that why you are angry? Now, let me ask you something. Does getting frustrated or angry help you get that jump, edge, spin? Of course not, you are just wasting energy. Why would you want to do something as crazy as that? Instead, relax yourself, shrug your shoulders and smile idiotically. Lie down on the ice for five minutes in a back spin position and play dead. Maybe somebody will trip over you and splatter themselves all over the ice.

Now that you know that being frustrated or angry does not help you the least bit, we can continue. If you don't get something (be it a spin or jump), go back and review that particular item. Did you follow all the suggestions, or are you still trying to do your own thing? Now try again. If you fall, just get up and try all over again. I don't care how many times you fall or how black and blue your butt is from falling, you just get up and do it again. I must have fallen myself a gadzillion times before I got some items. So why are you so special to think that you need not fall? In fact, if you do not fall, it actually means that you are too afraid to fall and therefore, are not learning anything new. There is nothing to be afraid of. As you know by now, falls don't really hurt if you have the right technique. And if they hurt, so what? Just do it again, and again, and again. I guarantee you that you will get that item some day, provided you do not give up.

Giving up is the worst thing you can ever do with your life. It means that you are too weak to carry on, or you are overcome by self pity and refuse to carry on. In both cases, you have finally failed. You are KAPUT.

However, if you try again (despite falling a gadzillion times), and again, you can never fail. As long as you keep trying, there is NO failure. Every time you fall, you are one step closer or one fall closer to getting that jump (or spin). Therefore, don't even think about giving up or saying that you cannot do "that thing." You just try over and over again until you get it. I don't want to hear any of your lame excuses for not being able to do it. You do it and then you are allowed to speak again. If you break your leg, then you wait for it to heal and then you come back to the rink and try the jump again.

If you break your ribs, tape them up, and continue jumping. If you sprain and twist your ankle and your doctor tells you that you cannot jump for three months, you ignore that advice and jump as soon as possible. There are no excuses good enough for giving up.

You may think that the above suggestions are too harsh and that I don't care about you. Let me tell you something. If I really do not care about you, I will tell you that it is okay to give up, that it is okay not to push yourself, that you are a sweet young thing and that you don't ever have to try that jump again. Unfortunately, I do care about you and your skating, so you won't hear those things mentioned. Period.

-36-

Is It Really Impossible To Do This Jump?

Along your fabulous skating life, you may come across a jump which just seems impossible to do. Never mind what jump it is, it is just impossible for you to do it. You have tried a million times and fallen a million times.

What you have to do now is to sit back and evaluate this jump. So sit back, let down your hair, put up your feet, and read this chapter.

Let us say you have gotten stuck at the double Axel level. You say that this jump is IMPOSSIBLE! But let us analyze this - if the jump is truly impossible, then why are all those people whom you see on TV doing it? Why are some people at the rink doing it? You have gotten into a mental block in which you have to overcome. No jump is impossible, because all jumps are possible!

Maybe the skating rink that you are skating at is not at the highest level. You are the best skater there, so there is no pressure for you to do the double Axel. If possible, skate somewhere else where everybody seems to be doing triples. Therefore, you are now at the bottom of the ladder again, and that should provide you with added incentive to catch up to the other skaters. If you cannot skate elsewhere, then try to skate alone at your rink - so you compare yourself to yourself and not with other skaters.

Another thing you can try is to skate to objectives. This is my favorite. I set a timetable as to when I must get the double Axel or triple or whatever. So what you do is you give yourself two months to do the double Axel - no more! If you die trying it, well, at least you tried it. Also, plan to get all jumps way before competition so you are comfortable with the jump. If you are uncomfortable with a jump, putting it in competition just makes you so nervous that you will probably wet your pants. Be absolutely comfortable with all the jumps in your program way before competition rolls around. So plan to land the jump, say one month before the competition. You have no choice now, you must land the jump or you cannot compete at that level.

Next, after getting rid of the mental block, you have to be physically capable of doing the jump. Are you skating fast enough on the entry into the jump? If not, skate faster. What is your excuse now? Are your shoulders and arms strong enough to do the fast revolutions necessary for the jump? If not, go develop some upper body strength. Go do those exercises which I have described before. What is your excuse now? Are you technically correct in the jump? Is your body straight while spinning in the air? Are your shoulders level? Is your right shoulder being forcefully thrown up and around on take-off? Are you flying backward straight? If not, go reread the technique for the jump. What is your excuse now? Are you getting too fat to spin faster? Are you a glutton for junk food? Are you a skating elephant? Then stop overeating immediately. What is your excuse now? Are you afraid of the jump? Go back and read those chapters again and again on fighting fear and reconditioning your mind. What is your excuse now? Are you too dumb to understand what I am trying to tell you? Then go back to school and be less dumb! What is your excuse now?

-37-

The Triple Jumps

If you are doing all your triple jumps right now, you are already at Olympic levels. When you get your first triple, you will not be able to sleep for a week. Your desire to get back to the rink and do ALL the triples will drive you crazy. And you will drive everybody around you crazy too!

However, to be prepared for competition at this level, you must be consistent in all of your triples. You cannot "get-it-one-day" and "lose-it-the-next-day." You cannot be a champion that way. Go back to that chapter on toughening up your mind and toughen up your mind.

When you prepare for your triples, remember you have to start to spin or twist while still on the ice. As stated before, if you are already up in the air without starting the spins yet, you will not get the triples. Also, try to enter the jumps with as much speed as possible. You will actually slow down the entry involuntarily when doing the triple Axel, but try to fight this involuntary slowing down. Many times, when you enter the triple jumps fast, you will fall down and slide backward in a straight line. BUT that is okay! What you are doing is getting rid of that fear of entering the jumps fast.

The arms must now fold in faster and tighter around the chest. You do not lift up your arms as much as in the double jumps. The free leg also folds in faster and tighter. You do not lift this free leg up too much either. In other words, you are getting into that back spin position as fast as possible. You want to get into that back spin position as soon as possible to get maximum revolutions! Make sure you use that right arm and shoulder to punch you around and up violently. Also, make sure your armpits are closed, and your left leg is crossed straight down on your right leg. It is absolutely crucial that you close yourself up as much as possible for the fast spins required to complete up the triples. Do not fear that you will over-rotate. That rarely happens. You need all the spins possible, so rotate as fast and as tight as possible.

(Yes! You are right again. This is another blank page.)

The Triple Salchow

This is the first triple jump to learn, and it is the easiest.

1. Hold this position. I repeat, hold this position and make sure your body is straight. If you lean over now, your jump will be tilted and you will fall when you land.
2. Spin violently as you are jumping straight up. The spin must take place now as you are jumping straight up. It cannot happen once up in the air. Make absolutely sure that your body and legs are straight as you spin on your way up. Also, remember that you have to jump "out there" so your landing is about 4-5 feet away from your take-off point. It has to be in a straight line "out-there."

3. Make sure your left leg is straight down in front of your right leg.
4. Make sure your armpits are closed.
5. Land.

The Triple Loop

1. Hold this position. I repeat, hold this position.
2. You must spin as you jump straight up and backward. Spin violently with both shoulders and hips as you take off. Remember, do not spin just the shoulders without spinning the hips. Otherwise, you will get bent like a pretzel and break at the hips and then fall. Make absolutely sure that every molecule of you is straight when spinning. Close your arms and legs the moment you go up to maximize revolutions. You cannot over-rotate, so do not be afraid of over-revolutions.

3. Make sure your left leg closes straight in front of your right leg immediately.
4. Land.

The Triple Flip

This jump is easier than the triple loop, as the right toe-pick assists you in climbing up much higher. However, you have to fight the tendency to lean forward too much when placing in that toe-pick. Remember you are flying backward in a straight line off that right toe-pick.

1. Reach back with that right arm for maximum explosion. Once again, make sure you do not lean forward too much or you will never be straight when you start to spin.
2. Spin both shoulders and hips around together violently the moment the toe-pick digs into the ice. Remember, you are jumping in a straight line backward off your right toe-pick. You must move in a straight line backward. So pick in straight back with your right toe-pick, not to the side.

3. Make sure your left leg closes straight in front of your right leg immediately.
4. Land.

The Triple Lutz

You will find this to be an easy triple if you go into the jump fast. This jump is very hard, to impossible, if you are moving slowly when you take off. Once again, remember that you have to fly backward in a straight line off the right toe-pick. (Although you have to take off on a back outside edge, think straight backward). Once again, try to do this jump way before you hit the boards. I have had some spectacular falls into the wall from being too close to the boards before jumping. Believe me, you don't want that to happen to you. Give yourself room to fly backwards.

1. Curve into that back outside edge as you reach way back with your right arm. Do not lean forward too much as you pick in.

2. Spin shoulders and hips around violently the moment the toe-pick digs in. Make sure you are already spinning when jumping up vertically off your toe-pick. You have to violently thrust the shoulders backward and around, so that you can spin straight and fast. You have to thrust backward forcefully because that is the only way to get your shoulders to catch up with that right toe-pick (which is straight behind you). Otherwise you will not be straight when you spin.
3. Land.

The Triple Axel

Although this jump is never as high or as far as the other Axels, it is the scariest. Think of it as a Do-It-Or-Die jump. You need this jump to win, so just do it.

1. Step into a big, deep outside edge and explode upward and around simultaneously. There will be a big skid mark on the ice, otherwise you are not spinning around as you are climbing up. Jump out in a straight line to get that additional split second to complete up that third revolution.

2. Fold in your legs and arms as fast as possible the moment you take off. You do not lift the free leg very high because you must start the spin right now! You must fold in the arms right now too.
3. Land.

The Triple Toe Loop

1. Land from a triple Axel and then reach back with your left toe-pick. Remember to reach back in a straight line and not to the side. Keep your body as straight as possible while bending your right knee deeply. Also try to keep that left arm in front of you for a second before spinning violently around and up. You keep that left arm in front (and the right arm behind) so you can spin around more violently.

2. Spin around violently with both shoulders and hips together. When you take off, you are facing forward already. Cross your legs and arms as fast as possible, immediately after take-off. Do not let your arms or your left leg be open too long. That prevents you from spinning immediately at take off. Remember also that you are going to travel about 2-3 feet backward in a straight line (never a curve).
3. Land.

-38-

Do You Know What I Am Talking About?

Let us get this straight. When you are doing all your jumps, you MUST jump up and spin AT THE SAME TIME. That means you are already spinning as you are still climbing up to the peak of your jump. At the peak of you jump, you have already done the first two revolutions. As you are coming down from your jump, you do the third revolution.

You must NEVER just spin without the jump up part. If you do, you will twist your upper or lower body and start to bend forward. Furthermore, there will be absolutely no height on your jump which gives you no time to complete up your triple revolutions. Even if you pull off the miracle of doing a triple jump a half-inch off the ice, you will never get the excitement of spinning fast four feet up in the air.

The other thing which you must remember is not to just jump up with no spin. If you jump up without forcefully spinning your shoulders around, you will just jump up very high. While it is indeed spectacular to jump up very, very high, you will find there is nothing up there to help you spin. The best that you can ever do when you pull your arms and legs real tight is a double jump. Many times, you will not even be able to do a double because you will open up completely and do only a single. In other words, you will do a six-foot high single Lutz, instead of a triple Lutz, and that is NOT going to win you any gold medals.

I have had coaches who told me to jump up (with no spin) and other coaches who told me to spin (never mind about the UP). Nothing worked at all, until I discovered that I had to jump up and spin at the same time. (Of course, you must spin your shoulders and hips at the same time as you are jumping up). So, would you rather pay a million dollars in ice-time fees or listen to my advice?

-39-

Stay Focused Or Else

There are many of you, myself included, who like many sports. We may even be at competitive levels in several sports. There is absolutely nothing wrong with liking and playing several sports, but unfortunately, if we want to win the gold medal at the Olympics - then we have to give up other sports to concentrate all of our energies on just one sport. That is what focus is all about. You put your whole mind into just one thing.

Let us say that you really want to be a very, very good skater. You even want to win at the next Winter Olympics! However, you also want to be a very, very good gymnast, and win at the next Summer Olympics. Now your mind is split in two. Half your mind is on skating and half your mind is on gymnastics. Your problem here is that there are many other people out there who will be competing against you who have put their WHOLE mind into either skating or gymnastics! Therefore, your half mind is competing with their whole mind. Who do you think will win?

I am not trying to tell you to do nothing else beside skating. In fact, you should do other things like bicycling, ballet, aerobics, etc. to strengthen your skating finesse. But you cannot over-dilute yourself to pursuing several sports at the Olympic level. Chances are that you will never become really good at anything. If you try to do everything, you will end up being good at nothing.

Just remember, concentrate on skating and focus on the gold medal. Have fun with other sports, but do not take them to the same level of intensity as skating. You will find yourself progressing much faster toward your goal if you stay focused.

-40-

Come Here And Rest Awhile, You Beautiful Thing

Sometimes, even after all the motivation, strength-training, and technique-refining, one jump just seems impossible. Remember, it is really not impossible. It just seems impossible for NOW. You are not alone. I have had many days just like that. What you have to do is to actually back off for just awhile and take a rest from that particular jump. It is not worthwhile to get all frustrated and angry everyday just because a jump seems impossible for the time being. I call this jump-burnout. You get so bogged down with that jump that it saps your vitality and enthusiasm. Do what people do when they have burnout. Have a short vacation. You will forget nothing in this 2-3 days off from the ice. This very mini-vacation will energize you and refill you with renewed strength and vigor.

The main thing is not to get frustrated and fly off into bad tempers or throw tantrums. It does not help your skating the least bit. Furthermore, looking sulky and moody just destroys your good looks. Stop and take a look at yourself in the mirror. See that beautiful person looking back at you. That's you! Why would you be so stupid as to destroy that beautiful person in the mirror just because of a jump? Just like many other people around you, I would love and accept you regardless of whether you can land the triple Axel or not. Those people are your true friends. The people who would only love and accept you if you land the triple Axel are NOT your true friends. You see, they do not really like you as you are but they like what you can do. You do not need friends like that. Remember, you cannot pick your family and relatives, but you sure can pick your friends. Once again, if you are suffering from a bout of burnout, re-read this chapter and know that there are people just like myself who would accept you just as you are!

Now that you are warm and fuzzy and coddled, SURPRISE! Your mini-vacation just ended. Now, please get back to the ice and double your efforts in getting the triple Axel. And I will skate right by your side and together we will do it!

-41-

Other Jumps

I have lumped together all other jumps into this chapter. They are relatively easy when compared to the triple jumps. Hence, I always think of these jumps as enjoyable, where the risk of falling is practically nil. In other words, you can do these jumps with a big smile on your face.

The Stag Jump

Approach this jump just like you are going to the single Flip jump. I like to do this jump going fast. The moment you dig in your right toe-pick, swing around, and jump straight up into the stag position. Just bend the left leg at the knee so that your calf muscles touch the hamstring muscles, and stretch that right foot straight back. Make sure you have some momentum to cover as much ice as possible. This allows you to hang longer in the air. Arch your back and point your right foot diagonally back straight. You just bend your left knee up to create the illusion that you are jumping a great height. Land this jump on the forward left toe pick. When you land, push your left arm forward forcefully. Then ride off on your right foot inside edge.

The Split Jump

The entrance into this jump is again like the single Flip jump. The moment you dig in the right toe-pick, swing the left foot around forcefully as you propel yourself up with your right toe pick. Do this jump fast and you will find it to be much easier. It takes a short while to get your two legs to be completely straight in the air. Once again, think about covering as much ice as possible and you will get a fabulous split. If you just jump up without covering much ice, it does not look that spectacular. Land as the Stag jump.

The Normal Russian Split Jump

Try to do this jump off-ice first, so you can get the feeling of splitting completely. Instead of swinging the left leg straight through now as in the normal split, I think of jumping up more straight into the Russian split position. Think of touching your toe-picks to your fingers and keeps those knees straight. Make sure you point the toe-picks as you split. Keep your body as straight as possible, while jumping up. Once again, try to cover as much ice as you can before landing on your left toe-pick.

Russian Split Jump With Open Hips

The Russian Split Flip

Here is a jump which I think everyone should learn immediately after learning the Russian Split. I find that this jump is actually easier because you land backward (instead of forward). Do everything exactly the same as the Russian Split. The moment you dig your right toe-pick into the ice, jump up and split as fast as possible. You have to split faster because you must rotate around more in order to land

backward. If you split too slow, you will find this jump to be impossible. That is because you do not have time to do that extra rotation to land backward. Once you hit the Russian Split position, immediately fold in your arms and drop your legs. The folding in of your arms will make you rotate so that you will land backward.

I found it easier to land this jump if I drop my right shoulder down as I drop my legs. But this does not look so good, so try to avoid it if you can.

The Russian Split Lutz

This jump is more spectacular than the split Flip, especially if you are going fast. Actually, I have never seen it done by anyone going slow, yet. Try to learn this jump as you are learning the split Flip. Everything is exactly the same except the entrance. Take off like a Lutz Jump and make absolutely sure to look up when you take off. If you look down, try to split and then land backward, you will fall and splatter your guts all over the boards. They will have to take an ice-scraper to scrape you off the boards! So make sure you look up when doing this jump!

The Delayed Axel

You must be able to do this jump before you do the next jump (the Open Axel). You will feel that you are "flying" when you do this jump well. There is nothing frightening about this jump. It is completely exhilarating and you will be on "high."

1. Take off just like you are doing a Waltz jump. Remember, jump in a straight line.
2. When you jump up, keep your head up and split your legs completely apart. I think of jumping on to the top of a high pedestal or box and landing on that box with my right foot. Keep your head looking straight ahead until you land on the top of that imaginary box. Do not spin at all until you land on the top of that imaginary box.

3. The moment you land on the top of that box, fold in your arms and legs and start the rotation.
4. Land.

The Open Axel

Here is one of the most spectacular jumps ever. You must do this jump with great speed and with absolutely no fear. It is just an ordinary Axel with the legs wide open (just as in a waltz jump) and the arms very slightly closed. You rely purely on power and height for the revolution. If you can do this well, you will frighten every other skater on your ice-rink.

1. Take off just as in a Waltz jump. Your right leg must swing around more quickly than in the delayed Axel. If you keep the right leg going out straight it will be impossible to spin around (because you are NOT folding in your arms or legs).
2. Hold this open position throughout. You can control the open position of the legs by concentrating on your stomach muscles. Keep your whole body weight centered squarely between your legs. Do not bend over.

3 Travel 12 feet across the ice in this open position. You can close your arms very slightly. However, the more open your arms, the more spectacular the jump.

-42-

Are You Mentally Prepared? Or Are You Brain Dead?

There is only one method to be mentally prepared before skating a perfect program. That method is called visualization. You must be able to use this technique if you want to achieve perfection in skating.

Close your eyes and visualize yourself going through your whole skating program. It must be from start to finish. Every detail must be in this picture. Where is your head? Where are your hands? Where is your body? Where are your legs? Where are you on the ice? Run through the whole program in your head. You must be able to visualize it in the same amount of time it actually takes you to do the actual program. Every jump must be visualized at exactly the same speed - as though you are actually doing it. You must not slow down the mental pictures in your mind. If you are visualizing a triple Lutz, then that triple Lutz must happen in your brain in less than one second. Because that is the time it takes you to do that on the ice. You cannot slow the triple Lutz down in your brain, otherwise visualization is a waste of time. Do this visualization process a thousand times before the competition itself.

Make sure that you put in ALL the details in the visual picture. You must visualize yourself in the clothes that you are going to wear. You must visualize the hardness of the ice, or the smoothness of the ice. You must visualize the smell of the ice. You must visualize the lights. You must visualize the crowds. You must visualize the noise that they will be making. You must visualize the silence. You must visualize the competitors. You must visualize the time of day. You must visualize how you will be feeling. In short, make it as detailed as possible.

Do this visualization process every day, as many times as possible. When it has sunken into your brain, you will be mentally prepared - finally. I find this to be the only effective method to deal with pre-competition jitters. Follow it and you will get calm too.

-43-

How Is Your Belief In Yourself?

Ultimately, after all the practice, after all the training, after all the nutrition, the best skater will be the one who believes that he/she is the best skater. That belief in yourself as Number One is crucial to winning.

There is actually not that much difference, physically, between top athletes. All are extremely well conditioned. All can do complicated footwork. All can do the triples. All can spin perfectly. But not all of them believe that they are Number One.

You must believe in yourself as Number One, or you cannot be Number One. There is so much pressure in skating that most skaters get mentally defeated before the competition actually begins. They will say, "Oh, well! Even if I am last, it is okay!" Actually, the truth is that it is not okay to be last - in your mind. That is, you must think and skate like number one before the competition. Your brain MUST accept the fact that you are number one. You will do everything perfectly. There will be no mess ups. You will look beautiful out there. There will be nobody as good as you. You have put in thousands and thousands of hours. So why shouldn't you be Number One? Never ever think that you are not as good as the other skaters. And don't ever let anybody tell you that either.

Now go out there and skate like the champion that you are. Skate like you are ALREADY Number One. Let me repeat, skate like you are already Number One!

-44-

What Do You Mean, You Cannot Do It?

Exactly what do you mean when you say you cannot do this jump? There is no such thing as not being able to do the jump. Yes, you CAN do the jump. Go back and review the technique again.

Are you approaching the jump with enough speed? What are you? A skating tortoise? Go get more speed!

Are you standing up straight before the jump? Are you trying to spin horizontally when you take off and bust all your ribs and face?

Are you spinning around violently using both your shoulders and hips at the same time? Or are you just spinning your shoulders and getting all twisted up in the air? Are you absolutely sure that you are straight in the air when spinning up there? If not, use your right arm and shoulder more forcefully next time. Spin that right shoulder and arm more violently up and around next time. What did you say? You are not strong enough!? Then go back to the chapter on working out and go build up stronger shoulder and arm muscles.

Are you doing everything correctly but still missing that one-quarter revolution? Well, close your arms and legs tighter, or do I close them for you permanently? You probably are bending your left knee and it is not straight such that an elephant can pass through that opening. Your armpits are probably open, too. Yes, I know you use SURE deodorant, but you are not doing an advertisement for them right now. Keep them closed tight.

Where is your head? Are you looking down? You look down only if you want to smash your face on the ice. Otherwise, look up and over your left shoulder. Think about keeping your chin up.

What? You are afraid!!? Just remember, you are an ice skater and you have NO FEAR!

-45-

All, I Mean All The Spins

Spins are extremely beautiful when done well. They are also much easier to do than, say, the triple Lutz jump. If you follow the suggestions here, you can get all your spins in less than one year. And that is assuming you are starting from nothing! Most of that one year will be spent on centering the spin on your left leg or your right leg. Once you can spin dead-center on your left leg or right leg, then you can get the next 20 spin positions in a few weeks.

If you have never spun before, the first few spins will give you a headache. Make sure you have some aspirin or Tylenol beforehand. The only way to get rid of that headache and dizziness is to do a million spins. The more spins you do, the less dizzy you get. After a few months, you will never feel dizzy ever again unless you stop skating for a long period of time and then try to reach competitive levels again. Even then, the dizziness will disappear after 1-2 days of spinning. One of the spins, called a layback spin, will make you nauseous for the first couple of days, even after you are a good spinner. I took about six aspirin tablets every day for three days before my head finally felt like it was attached to my body again. However, once you get it, it is one of the most beautiful spin positions imaginable.

So, are you ready to become the beautiful "spinner" that you always knew you were? If yes, pay careful attention to the next couple of pages and in a short period of time, you will become the most beautiful spinner in your ice-rink.

The Two-Foot Spin

You do this spin for only one purpose, and that is to get used to spinning. Once you get used to it, quickly move to the next spin. Do not spend too much time perfecting this spin because it is not very important.

1. Just stand up straight with both feet underneath you. You can put your feet close together. Put your left arm in front of you and your right arm behind you.
2. Wind-up by twisting your shoulders to the right. Your right arm is now way behind you, ready to swing around. Your left arm is still in front of you. Bend both knees, and look straight ahead.
3. Throw your right arm around and stand up straight in one go. Make sure you keep your legs close together as you start to spin. Keep your chest up and your tummy in. Keep your chin up too. To spin faster, close your arms to your chest with your elbows touching your ribs. Do not bend at the waist. Just stand up straight and spin.

The Scratch Spin

This is the hardest spin to learn but once learned, you can do any spin. So do a million of this spin before doing anything else. The only way to do this spin well is to do it until you are absolutely sick of it. There is no other way.

1. Do a backward crossover until you are standing straight on your right back inside edge. Your left arm is in front of you and your right arm is behind you in the wind up position. Keep your upper body straight while bending deeply with the right knee.
2. Now, step wide back to where you came from with your left foot forward outside edge. You must step back into the circle. You must bend your left knee deeply. You must step into a forward outside edge. Do this slowly. Do not hurry. Throw your left arm and right leg around violently the moment you hit the three-turn. The moment you hit the three-turn, stand up straight and you will start to spin.

(continued over)

3. You are now in the spin position. Keep your right foot extended perpendicularly in front of you as you spin. Your arms are at ribcage level. Spin slowly here. You may have to actually slow down your spin here so that you can center the spin. Be relaxed and do not hunch up your shoulders. Keep your body straight and your chin up. Do not spin on your toe-pick. Instead rock back away from the toe-pick to the ball of your foot.
4. Once you feel centered, bring in both your arms to your chest and cross your right foot over your left foot slightly above the left knee in one go. You will begin to spin really fast now. As you feel comfortable, push both arms and free leg downwards. Now you will become a blur - the closest to becoming invisible!

To Exit the Scratch Spin

1. Bring your right foot close to your left foot.
2. Step onto the right toe pick and into the back outside-edge. At the same time, push backward with your left leg inside edge. Also, open up both arms to your side.
3. Ride backward on the right foot by swinging the left leg backward. Bend the right knee deeply. The left leg must be straight, no bend at all. Hold this position.

The Attitude Spin

As you are doing the Scratch Spin, you can try an Attitude Spin by bending the right leg at the knee and putting the whole right foot (inside edge facing the ice) behind you. Make sure you hold the right foot up high above the ice. Push your hips squarely out. Continue spinning on your left foot.

The Back Spin

You had better get used to this spin because you have to do it your whole skating life. Do this spin whenever you get to the rink as a warmup.

1. Skate on a left forward inside edge. Bend the left knee deeply. You can stretch the right foot behind you before bringing it in close to your left foot.
2. Step onto a deep right forward inside edge. Bend your right knee deeply. You are going to do a back three-turn to start the spin. Keep your body straight.
3. The moment you do the three-turn, swing your left leg and left arm around forcefully. You also have to swing the right arm around. As you start the spin, your arms are out to your side and your left leg is parallel to the ice (straight out diagonally in front of you). You must stand straight here - in fact, arch your back a little bit. Look over your left shoulder with your head.

(continued over)

4. Now spin really, really fast on the flat of your blade by closing your arms to your chest and lowering your left leg straight down your right leg. Press the heel of your free foot down. You must spin fast because this is THE POSITION for all your triple jumps. You must be able to spin fast, otherwise say bye-bye to your triples.
5. To exit, open up your arms, lift up and then swing forcefully your left foot backward. Bend your right knee deeply to ride out on a back outside edge. Practice this exit until you can do it perfectly. This is the same exit position for ALL your jumps.

The Sit Spin

Enter this spin like the Scratch Spin. Make sure you go all the way down in this spin, otherwise it does not look good. All the way down means your calf muscles must touch your hamstrings when spinning in the sit-spin position. You must go down during the first spin. Never wait.

1. Step forward on the outside edge, just like in the scratch spin. Make sure your body is straight and your head is looking up.
2. Spin and throw that free leg around forcefully, and GO DOWN in your first spin. Do not delay going down! Make sure your throw your left and right arm around forcefully.
3. Throw the free leg around with the inside edge facing upward.
4. Go down all the way. Stretch those arms forward in front of you for balance. Do not hold your free leg. And look up straight in front of you. Make sure your free leg inside edge is facing upward toward the ceiling. This free leg MUST be straight out in front of you. Keep your body straight without hunching over.

The Reverse Sit-Spin (Change Sit Spin)

Without getting up from the normal sit-spin, open up your arms, step over from left foot to right foot (without getting up or changing positions!), close your arms forcefully, and start spinning on your right foot outside edge sit-spin position. Be inventive with your arms. Cross them, or put one in front of you and the other behind you and look down. Make sure you go all the way down in this reverse sit-spin position. It does not look good if you do not go all the way down.

The Layback Spin

This is the most beautiful spin you can do. So make sure you do not mess this spin up! Enter the spin like you are going to do a fast scratch spin. Next, center the spin. You must center the spin first before doing the layback, otherwise you will start to travel across the ice. Once centered, lift your right leg into an attitude position -with the inside edge facing the ice. In one go, push forward your hips and lean back with both shoulders. Make absolutely sure that you lean back with both shoulders so that they go backward at the same level. If you lean back with only one shoulder, your layback spin will not be a beautiful spin. You will find that you can lean back more the more you push your hips out in front of you. So push those hips out. Your head should drop way backward so that you can see everything behind you! Arch your back until it hurts. Your chest should face the ceiling when you are properly arched. As for your hands, you can hold them upward or stretch them out to the sides. Or you can try some other position for your arms.

The Cross-Foot Spin

This is a difficult two-foot spin to perfect. It is easy to learn, but hard to perfect. Do a fast scratch spin on your left foot and then just put your right foot down (slightly apart from your left foot) on the ice. Now you are spinning fast on two feet, on the inside edges. Now here's the tough part. Standing perfectly straight, with an arched back, slide and cross your left foot over your right foot. Both feet remain on the ice throughout this sliding and crossing-over motion. I find that if I put more weight on the right foot, it is easier to cross the left foot over. Now put the palm of your left arm on your tummy and the back of your right palm on the back of your lower spine. Continue spinning fast, and you will amaze everybody!

The Camel Spin

This is quite an easy spin if you keep your chin and left shoulder up and arch your back. If you drop your head and left shoulder, you will find this spin to be impossible.

1. Do backcrossovers to enter into the spin. Step back into the direction you came from, bending the left knee deeply to do the forward outside edge. Do a deep, deep, forward outside edge on your left foot. Keep your body straight, and your right leg behind you.
2. The moment you hit the three-turn, straighten up your left foot and sweep around violently to the left with your left arm, left shoulder and head. Make sure your head is looking up and do not drop your left shoulder. Only now does the right leg straighten up straight behind you. Arch your back until it hurts. Stretch the right leg behind you until it hurts. Put your right arm behind you as you spin.
3. When you are spinning fast, you can now bring your left arm down and touch your left knee. You still do not drop your left shoulder or head, though. Try to spin on the outside edge of your left foot.

Other Camel Spin Positions

In this position, hold out your left arm straight in front of you and then purposefully look down at the ice. Make sure the left shoulder is not dropped. Keep it high.

When your Camel Spin becomes really good, try the semi-layover position. As you roll your body over, make sure that you hold your head and right leg up high. You will immediately lose the camel position if you lower either your head or right leg. You need strong stomach and back muscles to hold this position.

The Low Camel Position

As you are spinning the regular camel spin, you can start bending your left knee deeply to do a Low Camel Spin. This is very easy if you continue holding your head and right foot up. Try not to spin too much on your toe-pick. Remember, arch your back until it hurts. If it does not hurt, you have not arched enough!

The Catch-Foot Camel Spin

Here is another simple twist to the basic Camel Spin. As you are doing the Camel (back arched, arched, arched), bend at the right knee and simultaneously reach back with your left hand to grab the blade of the bent right foot. Remember, keep your head up. After doing it a few times, you can reach back and grab that blade automatically (without ever needing to look back to find your blade).

The Flying Camel Spin

This is an easy Camel Spin. Remember to always keep looking up and keep that back arched. Do not jump too high on this spin as you will lose the back camel position when you land.

1. Do backcrossovers, step forward (in the direction you came from) just like you are going to do an ordinary camel spin. Keep your chin up. Keep the left shoulder up all the time. The right shoulder is pressed down and behind you. Bend the left knee deeply, doing a deep, deep outside edge.
2. From the bent left knee, jump around (not up) and try to be parallel to the ice for a split second before landing on a bent right knee. (It is like a waltz jump with your body parallel to the ice).
3. The moment you land, check with the left arm for one split second and then swing that left arm vigorously back and spin in a back camel spin position. Keep that chin up and that back arched. Arch that back until it hurts. You are spinning on a back outside edge.

Layover Back Camel Spin

Here is a tough Camel spin. After the landing of the Flying Camel, twist your whole body until your chest faces the ceiling. Your arms are now straight out by your side, as you look at the ceiling, in a Layover Camel position. The secret here is to keep your head and body parallel to the ice (even a little bit up). I find that the least bit of drop of my head will make me lose the position completely. You must also be able to spin on that back outside edge on your right foot or it will not work.

The Corkscrew Spin

This is an easy spin. From a fast scratch or back spin, bend your skating knee deeply (deeply, deeply, deeply) and put your other foot behind (at the knee with the toe-pick pointing down) your skating foot. You can put your arms out in front of you with palms up, or take up the position as shown (looking downward).

You can also put your free leg on top of your skating leg (just above the knee) and spin that way. The free leg toe-picks are pointed downward with the inside edge facing the ceiling. You can put your arms in the position as shown.

The Broken Leg Spin

Here is a very beautiful spin. Do a fast scratch spin. Center the spin. Immediately, drop down on your left leg just like in a sit-spin with your right leg bent and hanging out to the side. You must go down all the way on your left leg. There is no half-way position! The right leg does not touch the ice as you spin around on your left leg. Your head should look downward over your right shoulder. Your left hand can be stretched straight diagonally, with your right hand folded over your chest. Spin fast in this position.

The Catch Knee Spin

This is one of my favorite spin positions. Do a fast scratch spin. Center it. Bend your right knee and put it behind you. Reach back with your right hand and catch your bent right knee and pull the leg so that it is completely behind you. All this while, keep your head looking straight ahead and arch your back deeply. You can fold your left hand across your chest such that the palm of your left hand is resting majestically on your right shoulder. Spin forever in this position.

The Forward Catch-Foot Spin

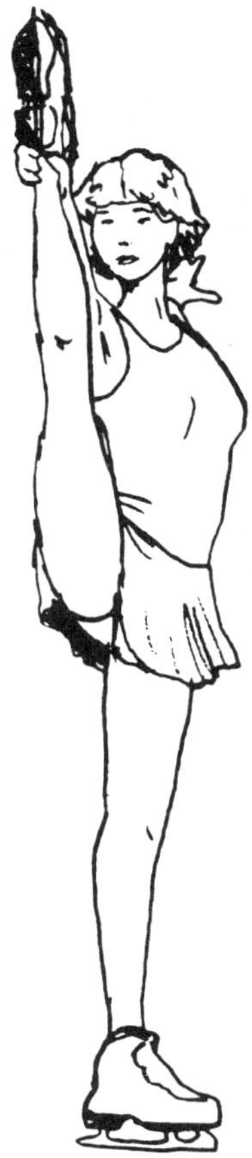

Do a fast scratch spin. Now reach down with your right hand (palms up) and catch the right foot at the ankle. Lift this right leg completely straight upward with your right hand. The right foot will swing a little bit to the side. However, try your best to not let this right foot swing too much to the side as it looks much better if you can let it stay at the front. Continue spinning on your left foot. Arch your back and head backward for balance. Put your left hand behind you for balance.

The Back Catch-Foot Spin

This is an easy and elegant spin. Do a fast scratch spin and then put your right foot behind you in attitude position. Reach back with your right hand (palms up) and catch the right foot blade at the middle. Now just lift the right foot up with your right hand. (You do not twist your right hand. Just lift it up.) Arch your back and head deeply as you tilt forward a bit. Stretch your left arm out to the side, and continue spinning elegantly.

The Bielman Spin

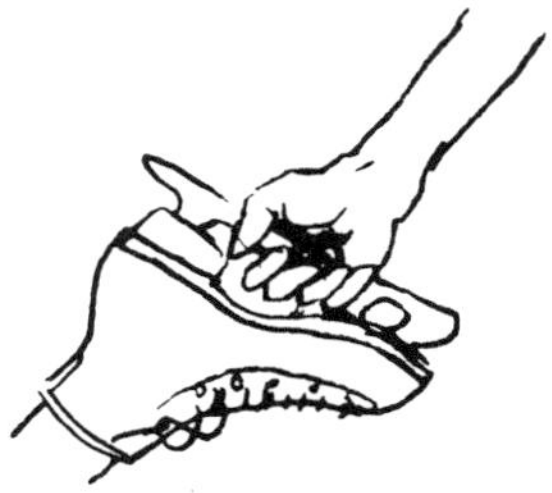

This is the hardest spin ever invented. I must have torn all the muscles in my right arm when I first learned it. Good Luck to You! Do a fast scratch spin with the right leg in attitude position behind you. Now reach back with your right hand (palms up) and grab your right foot blade in the middle. Now twist your right hand completely around to lift the right blade over and above your head. This twist of the right hand really hurts your right arm and back muscles. You must, at the same time, push your right shoulder forward so that the right hip does not twist back. Arch your back and head backward until it hurts. Once you hit this position, reach back with your left arm and grab the right fingers. With both arms lift the right leg completely straight up over your head. Now arch your head until it looks backward. You have the Bielman position! Continue spinning fast in this position.

The Flying Sit Spin

Think of entering the flying sit-spin like an Axel, and you will find it to be actually quite easy.

1. Do back crossovers. Just before the step into the jump, swing the left arm forward and the right arm backward.
2. Step into the flying sit spin just like you are going to do the Axel jump. Begin to spin around, such that you "skid" on the ice on take off.
3. Swing that right leg around forcefully, and leave it to the side. Do not swing the right leg in front of you. At the same time, jump straight up with your left leg, with your body straight. Make sure your arms are in front of you when you jump.
4. Immediately, as you are spinning around, try to touch your left knee to your chin. This is the flying sit spin in the air. The right leg is out to the side, not in front of you.
5. Straighten your left leg as you land on your left toe-pick.
6. Go straight down into a sit spin position by swinging the right foot around in front of you now.

The Death Drop Spin

Once again, think of the entrance to the Death Drop spin as going into an Axel jump. Approach this jump fast, otherwise it loses its dramatic effect. The entrance is exactly the same as in a flying sit-spin. However, the position in the air should be like a flying camel.

1. Spin around as you take off. There should be a "skid" mark on the ice as you are taking off. Now swing the right leg up and around forcefully. Unlike the flying camel, you must jump high up and around at the same time. Keep your back arched throughout.
2. Jump up and split those legs wide apart.
3. Turn over into the parallel position in the air.
4. Check firmly with your left hand as you prepare to land with your right toe pick. Let your left leg scissor around. Do not stop the momentum as this left leg helps you spin when you land.
5. Land on your right toe-pick and immediately go down into the reverse sit spin position. Close the legs quickly. Make absolutely sure you check with your arms and shoulders as you land. Otherwise you will lose the reverse sit spin. Also, never let the left boot hit the ice as you land.

-46-
Combo Spins

Too bad, I am not going to describe any combination spins to you! Why? Because you should be able to combine any spin together. If I can do it, so can you.

However, I have some advice for you. Look at your quad muscles again. Are you strong enough to do one spin after another without losing speed? If you do not have enough strength to do the first spin fast and you look dead already, surely you will die when you step into the next spin. Examine your stomach muscles. You must have something there other than fat. Otherwise, it is tough, tough, tough. And always arch your back and stand up straight. Do you have any back muscles?

Another piece of advice is to open up your arms when you step from one spin to another. The moment you step over into the second jump, close your arms again to get more speed (like a forward sit spin into a reverse sit-spin). If you jump from the first spin to the second spin, make sure you throw the arms and legs around forcefully (like a reverse camel into a forward sit-spin). If you just change spin positions all on one leg (like a sit spin into a Camel spin), make sure you hit the second position fast and throw that free arm around violently. That is the only way to get any speed at all on the second spin. And yes, it is hard to do a Camel spin after a sit spin.!

Want to get adventurous and try something? If yes, then try this spin combination.

1. Do a fast scratch spin (left leg)
2. Change into a layback spin (bend way, way back)
3. Change into a sit spin (drop down fast)
4. Change into a camel spin (up fast and swing that left arm forcefully around)
5. Jump over into a reverse camel spin (keep that back arched and your right leg straight)
6. Go down fast into a reverse sit spin
7. UP again into a reverse camel spin (swing that left arm)
8. Jump over into a forward sit spin (jump from the right foot straight up and swing both arms around forcefully and land on your left leg sit spin position)
9. Rise up and do a fast attitude spin
10. Now catch the right foot blade and pull up, with both arms, and do a Bielman spin
11. End with a left foot corkscrew spin (looking down)
12. Exit.

Did you get all of that? If not, go out there on the ice and start practicing harder.

-47-

Some Beautiful Glides OR How To Torture Yourself

Some of the most beautiful stuff you can do on the ice is to glide effortlessly in a particular position, while looking straight at the audience. Your arms will point at them, beckoning them enticingly, or embrace them with warmth.

Do all such glides at great speed and when you hit the glide position, maintain the position for at least 10 seconds. Never, never, never, ever rush a gliding position - even if you are going to do a triple Lutz at the end of your Spread Eagle. Hold that Spread Eagle position, then do the Triple Lutz.

Remember, arch your back deeply, keep your chin up and just glide! If it hurts, so what? The hurt will pass, but the beauty will always remain.

The Inside Spread Eagle

Here is an easy, beautiful Spread Eagle position. Using backcrossovers, skate fast backwards, and then suddenly step onto an inside edge with your forward or leading leg. The back leg is already in an inside edge. Your are now in a spread eagle position with your toes pointed out in opposite directions. Arch backward until your back hurts by pushing your hips out. Try to hold this position for about 20 seconds on a big circle. Your arms can be in the positions shown.

The Outside Spread Eagle

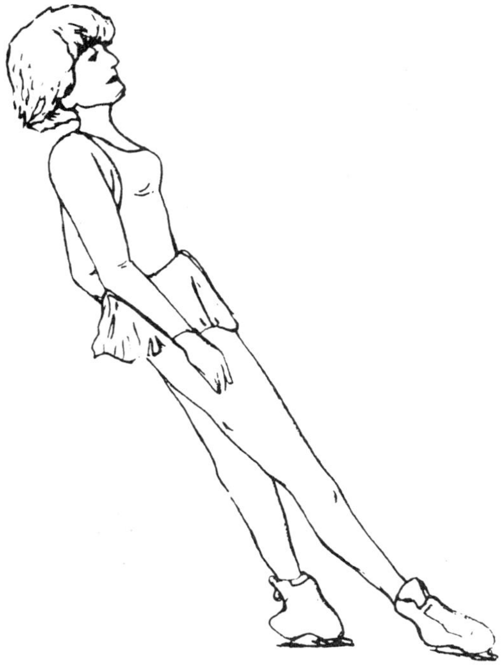

Here is a harder, more beautiful spread eagle. Using backcrossovers (anticlockwise direction), skate fast backward, and then suddenly twist around forward and step onto an outside edge with your forward or leading leg. Start to lean backward. This will automatically force the back leg to go from an inside edge to an outside edge. Dig your edges deep into the ice and really lean back now as you hold this position for about 20 seconds. You have to force your heels out if you want a good outside spread eagle. I like to arch my back when I lean back, thrusting the hips forward at the same time. If you go really fast, you can lean back at impossible angles. It is really, really beautiful.

The Back Pivot (using left toe-pick)

Here is an easy-to-learn pivot. Using backcrossovers, skate fast backward. Depending on which direction you are going, your right foot is either on an inside or outside edge. If on an inside edge, glide on it and turn into an outside edge. Now just stand on your right leg, going in a very big circle backward, on a back outside edge. Bend, the right knee deeply. All the weight of your body is on the right knee. There is no weight exerted on your left leg. As you are going in a big circle on your right back outside edge, put the left toe-pick ever so lightly on the ice. Remember, all your weight is on your right leg, none on your left. Just ride out the edge on the right foot. To end the pivot, I like to go down on my left knee and slide on the ice, with the right leg straight to the side (inside edge down facing the ice).

The Ina Bauer

Here is a classic ballet position which is extremely beautiful. Skate fast forward, and suddenly swing one leg straight out to the side behind you with the toe pointing backward. Look forward as you do this, otherwise you will lose the position. Do not look down or backward. Most of your weight should be on the forward foot. Bend the forward foot at the knee deeply. The more you can bend it, the more you can stretch the other foot out to the side. The forward foot can be on an inside edge, a straight edge, or an outside edge. The back foot is always on an inside edge. The most beautiful position has the forward foot on an outside edge. As you go in a big circle, arch your back and lean backward (still looking forward). If you have long hair, you can let your hair touch the ice as you lean back. It looks gorgeous.

The Spiral

You can do spirals forward or backward. You can do them on inside or outside edges. As long as you arch your back deeply (until it hurts), you will look good. If your back does not hurt you while doing the spiral, you are not arched enough yet. Make sure that your free leg is straight (no bend at the knee) and your toe-picks are pointed diagonally backward. To really do a fantastic spiral, I find that you have to push your skating foot out. That means it is not straight underneath you, but PUSHED OUT a little bit in front of you. Then you can really lift the free leg up high above and behind you. Your back will hurt, but so what? And always be careful not to trip over your toe-picks as you lift that free leg up higher and higher.

One-Foot Glides

You can do spectacular one-foot glides - straight into the audience's hearts. Arch your back deeply and skate directly toward the audience when you glide. Make sure you hold the positions for awhile so that everybody can see your grace and finesse!

Crossovers Glide

I like to do these glides from backcrossovers. Do fast backcrossovers, gather speed, and then gracefully stop the crossovers and hold the position. Bend your right leg deeply, and keep the left leg straight out to your side and a little bit in front. Hold the position as shown for a couple of seconds, and then resume crossovers or glide backward.

-48-

Down On My Knees

Here are a few of my favorite "down on my knees" lunges, fast slides, and positions on the ice.

I always try to hold the positions for a period of time so that it is clearly visible to everybody. Unlike the multiple revolution jumps where the jumps are not clearly visible to the eye because it happens so fast, these positions are meant to be held so that everybody can appreciate them.

Make sure that your head and arms are elegant as you do these moves. Otherwise, the whole effect will be marred. You should get "oohs" and "aahs" from the audience if you do it properly. If possible, try to slide straight across the ice while maintaining the positions.

Another trick which I learned was that while you are sliding fast across the ice in a straight line, if you turn your shoulders fast, you can turn your whole body (preferably on an outside edge of your leading foot, if any) so that you are now going backward - still holding the SAME position. It is spectacular! If you are going fast enough, you can turn your shoulders once again and go back to going forward! However, make sure that you have good ice while doing this, as I have scraped my knees black and blue on poor ice.

-49-
My Poses

Here are a few of my positions on the ice. I can use it at the start, in between, or at the end of the skating program.

Make sure you hold the position for awhile so that everyone can appreciate your stature and posture. It also helps you catch your breath when done in the middle of your program. And because of its elegance, nobody in the audience will suspect that you are actually recomposing your breath and mind to prepare for that final triple Axel before the end of your program!

Be sure to arch your back and point your fingers elegantly when holding such positions. Stretch those arms and legs and back muscles. It must look good!

Here are some transition poses where you hold the position for about 1-2 seconds before moving again.

-50-

My Spin Positions

After I had done all the classic spin positions, I invented some new spin positions. Some of the spin positions have to be practiced off-ice first in front of a mirror to make sure that the arm and leg positions are absolutely graceful.

I do some of the spins here with my left foot and others with my right foot. Some of the positions that you see here can only be held for approximately 3-4 revolutions. At least, that is the best I can do. But I try to do the 3-4 revolutions slowly so that everybody can clearly see the position. All of the spins here are actually part of spin combinations, meaning that you can do the classic spins first and then step into one of these new positions. I do the classic spin fast but slow down when trying these new positions.

I hope you enjoy my spin positions!

-51-

My Jump Positions

After learning all the classic jumps and all the triples, you may like to try some of my jump positions. These jumps assume that you can skate fast and then jump straight up into the air to strike a particular posture for 1-2 seconds.

As the jumps can be entered into in an infinite number of ways, I am going to leave you to figure out how best you want to enter into the jump. You can enter into some of these jumps just like in a Waltz jump. However, when you land you must be able to take off immediately from a forward landing position. In other words, you land forward and use the momentum to jump up into another position immediately. Some of the jumps can be performed like a half-Loop jump. Yet others, you can reach back with your left toe-pick and then jump up and land back again on your left toe-pick. Still other jumps can be done just like you are taking off from a Lutz jump, but instead of turning, you jump straight up and strike a posture. Many of the jumps can be done as combinations. For example, after landing from the Axel jump, you can reach back with your toe and jump straight up again into one of these positions shown.

Make sure your toe-picks are pointed downward or forward/backward diagonally when doing these jumps. Your hands should reach for the sky. Your body should be arched. Some of the jumps are very easy while others are very difficult. You must be able to jump off from either foot and land forward or backward. You can even do 1-2 revolutions in the positions shown. However, you must be able to skate very, very fast in order to do the revolutions because the arms and legs are not closed tightly around the body.

-52-

Grab The Popcorn And Turn On The TV

Actually, you are not supposed to eat any popcorn as it may fatten you.

One of the ways to get inspired in your skating life is to watch some of the skating programs performed by your favorite skaters. When you feel down about a jump or about ice-skating in general, pop a tape into your VCR, sit back, and watch power and grace unfold before your eyes. The beauty and magnificence of some skaters will reinforce why you are doing it in the first place. You will see a lifetime of dedication to the sport, the millions of hours of training, the tears shed in practice, the dreams of a lifetime - all compressed into a program a couple of minutes long.

At the very least, you must watch Brian Boitano, Elvis Stojko, Toller Cranston, John Curry, Scott Hamilton, Robin Cousins, Viktor Petrenko, and Kurt Browning. On the female side you must watch Midori Ito, Kristi Yamaguchi, Denise Bielman, Peggy Fleming, Dorothy Hamill, Katarina Witt, and Michelle Kwan. There are many, many more fantastic skaters that I have not mentioned here. These people have sacrificed many thousands of hours to bring the sport of ice-skating to new levels. If you watch Dick Button doing a flying sit-spin, it will send you away ashamed at your own skating level. If you watch Oksana Bauil doing her Swan Lake routine, you will cry.

And that is exactly what figure-skating is all about. Watch all these skaters, the sacrifices made, the pain suffered, and the beauty that lasts forever.

-53-

Stay Beautiful For Life

You have come to the end of this book now, but you are just beginning your stellar skating life. If you stay faithful to practicing the techniques described here, you will stay thin and beautiful for life. You have to skate often or whenever you can. Your skating abilities will give you thousands and thousands of wonderful, beautiful, graceful and happy hours. All the work that you put in will bless you with wonderful posture, a tough discipline, and a perseverance that will make you a successful person in life. But best of all, you can eat whatever you like and never grow fat!

As you grow older, you can become a fantastic coach to younger skaters who will look up to you. You have to be disciplined in order to give them discipline. You have to be good, to teach them how to be good. You have to be powerful in order to teach them how to be powerful. You have to be graceful in order to teach them grace. You have to be a beautiful skater in order to teach them how to be beautiful. But most of all, you must know the joy of ice-skating so you can share with them this joy. For only if you have it can you give it away.

May God bless you all.

YES!
YOU CAN DO THE TRIPLE JUMPS